I0802037

Delectable Destinations

Dedicated to my daughter, Emily Klein.
You are the sweetest part of my life.

Also by Deborah Reinhardt:

From Grief to Glory/A 30-Day Devotional Journey for People in Transition

Available at www.DeborahReinhardt.com

Delectable Destinations

A Chocolate Lover's Guide to Missouri

Deborah M. Reinhardt

Acclaim Press
MORLEY, MISSOURI

Acclaim Press
— Your Next Great Book —
P.O. Box 238
Morley, MO 63767
(573) 472-9800
www.acclaimpress.com

Book & Cover Design: M. Frene Melton

Copyright © 2016, Deborah Reinhardt/Girl Power Publishing, LLC
All Rights Reserved.

No part of this book shall be reproduced or transmitted in any form or by any means, electronic or mechanical, including photocopying, recording or by an information or retrieval system, except in the case of brief quotations embodied in articles and reviews, without the prior written consent of the publisher. The scanning, uploading, and distribution of this book via the Internet or via any other means without permission of the publisher is illegal and punishable by law.

All addresses, phone numbers and websites were correct at time of printing.

ISBN: 978-1-942613-28-2 / 1-942613-28-8
Library of Congress Control Number: 2015918610

First Printing: 2016
Printed in the United States of America
10 9 8 7 6 5 4 3 2 1

This publication was produced using available information. The author and publisher regret they cannot assume responsibility for errors or omissions.

Contents

Foreword

It's very clear Deborah Reinhardt left no stone – or truffle – unturned as she explored Missouri in her search for compelling stories and delicious creations to share with readers of *Delectable Destinations*.

While the subsequent pages showcase some of Missouri's tastiest creations, the real treat here is following Deborah's lead and her inspired writing on what's easily the sweetest path to follow around the Show-Me State.

On every page, unique slices of Missouri history unfold. Each chocolate maker has his or her own story and each chocolate shop's origin is fascinating.

Along the way, enjoy chocolate-centric tours of cities such as St. Louis, Kansas City and Springfield. Learn more about the people in history-rich communities such as St. Joseph and Ste. Genevieve. Visit Columbia, noted for its college-town vibe and creative personalities, and the charming wine-country community of Hermann, a great location for pairing wine with chocolates.

Although the emphasis is on chocolate, Deborah's work invites you to savor a collection of tasty morsels: chocolates made in a world-famous author's hometown, the imaginative souls behind a popular chocolate and beer pairing, and a small shop whose origins have a connection to Thomas Jefferson.

Yes, that Thomas Jefferson.

As your reading journey nears completion, another treat awaits. The compilation of recipes in the final section of this book is equal parts enticing and exciting. The ingredients you need to create a sweet indulgence at home are there; it's up to you to make it work.

Before confining yourself to the kitchen, let me invite you to follow in Deborah's footsteps and to visit Missouri's chocolate shops, and the communities they call home, for yourself.

When you travel in Missouri, you will find the fun activities waiting for you are as varied as a box of … well, you get the idea.

The Show-Me State is blessed to have beautiful outdoor resources, a diverse and exciting lineup of destinations and attractions, immersive cultural institutions, renowned live-show venues and performance halls, world-class restaurants and lodging establishments, wineries, breweries and so much more.

The opportunities for fun and memorable getaways are many in Missouri. When we at the Missouri Division of Tourism encourage people to Enjoy the Show, we're extending to them an invitation to enjoy the entire Show-Me State.

Even if it's just one taste at a time.

A heartfelt thanks to Deborah for bringing these Missouri stories into the spotlight. She no doubt considered every word … and enjoyed every bite.

– Dan Lennon, CDME
Director, Missouri Division of Tourism

Preface

I can't remember when I *didn't* love chocolate.

My earliest memory is from the second grade at Eliot Elementary School in St. Louis' Hyde Park neighborhood. My teacher knew I had an allergy to both milk and dark chocolate, so when it was time for her to make the little candy Easter nests for her students, I got the white chocolate Easter bunny.

"White chocolate" is a misnomer. Having no cocoa solids, this white couverture is really cocoa butter. While her efforts were appreciated, little wonder I felt something was missing in my Easter basket.

Because chocolate was the forbidden fruit for me growing up, it took on this mysterious quality, a sultry siren song that called to me, "Just take a bite." Sometimes I couldn't keep from it and savored the chocolate as I scratched the itchy hives popping out on my neck and face.

Thankfully, I've outgrown this food allergy, which, as an adult, has allowed me to eat and cook with chocolate.

I also love to travel, especially around my home state of Missouri, and I'm not alone. According to the Missouri Division of Tourism's annual report for fiscal year 2014, 39.2 million visitors either toured their home state or came to Missouri, resulting in an economic impact of $15.3 billion for the state. While in Missouri, 37 percent experienced unique or local dining, second only to shopping (42 percent) as a favorite vacation activity.

So, why write a book about Missouri and chocolate? Honestly, Missouri isn't the first state that comes to mind when thinking about the confection. Pennsylvania and Hershey, and California and Ghirardelli are known by far more people.

Actually, I simply thought it would be a fun project.

But as I researched the subject, interviewed chocolate makers, and traveled through Missouri, I discovered that the Show-Me State should show off its chocolate destinations. There are some incredibly talented artisans doing amazing things, not only with chocolate, but within their communities. Many of them left careers to follow their chocolate passions. Now, they are doing what they truly love to do. A few are even making a positive impact on folks in developing countries, and that truly is remarkable.

My thanks to all of those who gave generous chunks of their time to talk with me about their chocolate businesses. I'm grateful to the convention and visitor bureaus who helped me set up interviews and showed me around their cities. To the communications team at the Missouri Division of Tourism, my thanks for all of your help. I am grateful to my two editors – Annie Cosby and Ele Stewart – both of whom are talented and patient professionals.

While you're traveling around Missouri to sample its culinary offerings, make time to chat with these chocolate artisans and shop owners. You'll find all of them are highly dedicated and passionate about what they're doing, which is making life a little sweeter for all of us.

– Deborah Reinhardt

St. Joseph
Hannibal
Bowling Green
Kansas City
Columbia
St. Louis
Lake of the Ozarks
Ste. Genevieve
Springfield

Northern Missouri

Travel through northern Missouri and you will come across communities filled with rich histories and some surprising food finds, including a variety of chocolate treats. From truffles that are works of art to a candy tradition that dates to the 1870s, your sweet tooth and sense of adventure will be satisfied in this region.

Kansas City

It's an unexpected surprise to find one of the country's leading chocolatiers in a city known for its barbecue and jazz, but unexpected surprises help define Kansas City. At the Missouri-Kansas border, you'll find a city with a vibrant culinary scene, diverse artistic offerings and welcoming hospitality.

Kansas City receives frequent national rankings. In 2015, Thrillist – a digital media company geared toward men that focuses on food, drink, and travel – tapped Kansas City as one of seven Underrated American Food Cities. *Travel and Leisure* magazine placed Kansas City in the Top 10 American Cities to Satisfy a Sweet Tooth.

I heartily agree, because Kansas City's sweet tooth is deliciously layered with European influences, trailblazing ingenuity, and the good old American attitude of "let's get this done." Let me briefly illustrate.

Christopher Elbow, after working in the Las Vegas food industry, returned home to create some of the most artistic chocolate I've ever seen or tasted. I wasn't sure if I should wear it or eat it, but you can guess my final choice.

In a shop that looks like a princess's room, the new owners of Panache Chocolatier are giving this Country Club Plaza landmark a brand new look, as well as an expanded line of handmade chocolate.

Once more, the story of a European immigrant turns out well at André's Confiserie Suisse, a family-owned business that celebrates more than 50 years of tempting Kansas City residents and visitors with mouthwatering chocolates and pastries.

Kansas City, with its many affordable or free activities for families, is also home to Chip's Chocolate Factory in Crown Center. Visitors can watch candymakers churn out more than 40 flavors of fudge to the delight of children of all ages.

You can't talk about candy in Kansas City without including Russell Stover Candies, which has its headquarters here. Started by Russell and Clara Stover in 1923, the business started in Clara's kitchen grew to include 35 retail shops throughout the country and can be found in more than 70,000 drugstores, gift shops, and department stores in each state and in Canada.

What's also interesting about Kansas City is a spirit open to collaborations. For example, one of the largest specialty brewers in the Midwest, Boulevard Brewing Company, worked with Christopher Elbow to make its chocolate stout (which, by the way, makes an amazing beer float with chocolate ice cream). Likewise, The Roasterie coffee company has collaborated with André's to create wonderful coffee-flavored chocolate bars that are akin to having a party in your mouth.

Finally, an urban inn – Southmoreland on the Plaza – takes hospitality to another level with its outstanding food service that includes chocolate waffles, pixie chocolate cookies at night, chocolate zucchini bread, and more. It's a complete destination unto itself, and for the foodie who wants to visit Kansas City, this is the place to stay. For those in town for a romantic celebration, the Russell and Clara Stover room is a delightful choice.

Bowling Green

In 1919, Thomas Jefferson Bankhead, a great-grandson of President Thomas Jefferson, started Bankhead Chocolates. Today, the folks at Bankhead make their chocolate candies much like their founder did, and people in northeast Missouri have come to appreciate the craftsmanship, as well as the taste.

Hannibal

Dutch chocolate-maker Jacob Stam was dedicated to making fine chocolates, and that tradition is still alive more than 100 years later. From hand-painted chocolates to buttery caramels and truffles molded into whimsical shapes, Chocolaterie Stam is a delightful surprise in the little town that Mark Twain once called home.

St. Joseph

In 1876, doctors' wages didn't always stretch far enough to raise a family, so Dr. George Washington Chase and sons set up a fresh produce business and later a candy factory above their store. Soon, the demand for Chase's hand-dipped chocolates took over the produce store.

The family developed a new cherry and chocolate candy in 1918 – Cherry Mash – that would become the best-selling cherry candy bar in the country. It's still produced in this charming northwest Missouri city that is also known for a pretty interesting business venture: the Pony Express.

A spirit of adventure is a common thread that runs through the fabric of northern Missouri. You will discover something delightful around every turn.

André's Confiserie Suisse

Kansas City

Switzerland is the world's top chocolate-consuming country, with the average person in 2014 consuming almost 20 pounds, according to ConfectioneryNews.com. Americans, on the other hand, eat about half that amount, consuming chocolate only about twice a week.

More than 50 years ago, master pastry chef and *confiseur* (chocolate-maker) André Bollier had a dream to bring fine European chocolates and baked confections to the United States. Starting a business in Switzerland was expensive, but it seemed doable in America, especially since André's brother was already living in Kansas City, Mo.

So, in June 1955, André and his wife, Elsbeth, emigrated from Basel to the Midwest, and by October, he had opened his shop. But, according to grandson René Bollier, the Midwest palate didn't demand pastries and chocolates made with pure butter, whipped cream, and natural flavors and ingredients.

André went on to open a tea room serving light Swiss luncheons, hoping that would draw more people in, who in turn would purchase candies and pastries to take home. When the demand for chocolate took an upswing in the 1970s, sales at André's exploded, and son Marcel and his wife, Connie, joined André's in 1974 to spearhead the expansion of the chocolate department. Marcel and Connie's son, René, and his wife, Nancy, came on board in 2001, marking the third generation to work in the business.

While you can get authentic Swiss dishes like chicken and mushroom *vol-au-vent*, it's the handmade chocolates and pastries that shine brightest here. Look for champagne bottles made of chocolate filled with addictive chocolate-covered almonds dusted either in confectioner's sugar or cocoa powder.

In fact, those almonds are André's best-selling chocolates by far, according to René Bollier.

"We contract to buy about 40,000 pounds of chocolate a year, and half of that easily goes to the almonds," he says.

To make these seductive little treats, Bollier says they roast the almonds in large copper kettles, bringing the nut to a rich brown color. Meanwhile, sugar is added to the kettle, and it caramelizes to create a sweet ring around the almond. The nuts are then covered in milk or dark chocolate. Confectioner's sugar dusts the milk-chocolate almonds, while cocoa powder goes on the dark. Another twist adds a kiss of French sea salt to the nuts, while "Grand Cru" almonds are coated with premium, single-source dark chocolate.

While the almond-filled chocolate champagne bottle makes a memorable gift, the almonds are also sold in bags or boxes. Along with André's locations, almond lovers can find their treasure at a small selection of Kansas City retailers, including Halls Department Store and Best of Kansas City in Crown Center.

"I like the idea of wholesale, but I'd rather have people buying direct from us," Bollier says.

Beautiful to look at and better to taste, André's truffles are made with fresh dairy cream and Swiss chocolate with ganache centers flavored with champagne, Grand Marnier, cognac, raspberry, or dark chocolate. Bollier says they use locally sourced ingredients whenever possible and, sometimes, that leads to tasteful collaborations. A new item, whiskey cordials, are chocolate shells filled with a mini shot of J. Rieger & Company's Kansas City Whiskey. But be prepared – these may look innocent enough, but they pack a punch.

Bollier says the cordials were originally supposed to be a one-time offering for a special event, but André's soon realized they'd need to make more.

"Our chocolate and the whiskey balanced so well together. People were so enthusiastic about these, we decided to continue developing them with Rieger's logo on top of the chocolate," he says. "It has a totally liquid center that's like a whiskey explosion in your mouth when you bite into it, but the dark chocolate blends in for an incredible taste."

Another collaboration occurred in the mid-1990s with The Roasterie, a local coffee company. Owner Danny O'Neill worked with Marcel Bollier to develop a unique coffee blend just for André's. Longtime colleagues, the two had conversations about combining chocolate with coffee to make bars, and while O'Neill said all the credit goes to Marcel and René, the goal was to taste the coffee in the bars. It took several months to get the right blend and balance.

"Each coffee reacts differently to the chocolate," O'Neill says. "But chocolate and coffee … I mean, I can't get enough."

Bollier also fondly remembered the process of creating the bars.

"The whole process was so interesting. I ate an insane amount of dark chocolate during that period, but it was tons of fun," he says.

The first bar to be introduced was the Gotham Espresso, and later pairings followed, such as the bar made with Kenyan coffee that O'Neill says tastes a bit like a cherry cordial. Another discovery was that when organic, fair-trade Ethiopian Yirgacheffe beans are blended in 72 percent dark chocolate, they release a subtle blueberry taste.

Bollier, who trained for three years in Switzerland to learn the craft of Swiss chocolate-making, is happy to see more of their customers are choosing dark chocolate. He said 20 years ago, 80 percent of the chocolate sold at André's was milk chocolate. Today, 45 percent of chocolate sold is dark chocolate, and Bollier anticipates it will keep climbing.

"People are really interested in the intense flavors of dark chocolate, plus the reported health benefits of dark chocolate do not hurt," Bollier says.

Courtesy of André's.

In October 2014, a wine and coffee bar was opened at the tea room location near Country Club Plaza. Bollier said the expansion was something his family had wanted to do for a while, but they were waiting for the right time. With a new apartment development opening close to the tea room and the economy coming back, it finally seemed right.

"We've always thought that it would be an amazing addition to what we already do," Bollier says. "People have been very positive; it's going very well." Bollier added that they may soon start chocolate and wine tastings at the new wine and coffee bar.

Whatever is offered at André's, one can always be certain it will be of premium quality and taste.

André's Confiserie Suisse
www.andreschocolates.com

5018 Main St.
Kansas City, MO 64112
(816) 561-3440
Store hours are 7 a.m. to 7 p.m. Monday-Friday; 7 a.m. to 6 p.m. Saturday. Café hours are 7 a.m. to 7 p.m. Monday-Thursday; 7 a.m. to 9 p.m. Friday and Saturday. Lunch is served from 11 a.m. to 2:30 p.m. Closed Sunday.

André's Rivaz
4929 W. 119th St.
Overland Park, KS 66209
(913) 498-3440
Hours are 10 a.m. to 5:30 p.m. Monday-Friday; 10 a.m. to 5 p.m. Lunch is served from 11 a.m. to 2:30 p.m. Serving coffee and pastries before and after lunch.

A franchised location is in Denver, Colo., (303) 322-8871.

Connect with André's on Facebook, Twitter or Instagram.

TASTY TIDBITS

The Roasterie

The unmistakable aroma of coffee surrounds The Roasterie's factory on West 27th Street in Kansas City from the moment you get out of your car to your first step inside. This is where the magic happens for coffee lovers, and Danny O'Neill most definitely is a coffee lover.

That may be this week's understatement.

"I'm neurotic, compulsive about coffee," he says with a wide grin.

Since 1993, The Roasterie – a specialty coffee-roasting company – has provided coffee lovers, as well as restaurants, coffee houses, specialty grocers and such, with premium air-roasted coffee. The process, which O'Neill describes as a little like air popping popcorn, unlocks the original flavors and highlights the best of the beans, which come from more than 30 coffee-producing countries.

Air roasting uses exact temperatures to gauge when the coffee beans are finished. It also allows for beans to roast without much damage, unlike traditional drum roasters, which gauge the beans' color to determine when the process is finished.

Air-roasted coffee is cleaner, not bitter and has a smoother edge, O'Neill says. And anybody who drinks 20 cups of espresso a day should know what he's talking about.

O'Neill, who originally hails from Iowa, didn't drink coffee until he visited Costa Rica as a student.

"I drink an insane amount of coffee ever since," he says.

After school, O'Neill worked and lived in Seattle, Wash., and came to Kansas City via Omaha, Neb., in 1991. Wanting to start a business, he says coffee was the only idea he had, so he started experimenting in his basement.

"I was too uneducated to know any better," he says. "Thank God I didn't have all the facts."

Passion for his business is readily evident in O'Neill, who says he loves to do local collaborations. In addition to the André's joint venture, The Roasterie has also worked with Kansas City's famed chocolatier, Christopher Elbow.

In 2005, the two men met – of all places – in New York's Time Square. The idea of working on something together was tossed around, and the result is air-roasted Central American coffee blended with Elbow's dark chocolate.

The Roasterie also sells a Bavarian chocolate-flavored coffee.

Other collaborations have been done with Original Juan food company to make a barbecue rub and sauce, Fine Vines Artisanal Ketchup to make a coffee-infused condiment, and most recently with The Tasteful Olive to produce a coffee-flavored balsamic vinegar that is so good, you'll want to eat it by the spoon.

Bean buddies who want to learn more about what The Roasterie is all about can take free tours of the factory any day of the week by reservation. Learn about roasting, blending, and cupping coffee. There's also a café at the factory, as well as in Brookside, Mo., and Leawood, Kan.

The Roasterie factory is at 1204 W. 27th St. Just look for the vintage airplane on the roof. Visit www.theroasterie.com for more information or call (816) 931-4000.

Courtesy of Deborah Reinhardt.

Christopher Elbow Chocolates

Kansas City

Walking through the door of Christopher Elbow Artisanal Chocolate in Kansas City's Crossroads District is a pivotal moment for any chocolate lover. The space, artfully simple in its design, seems to have been made to pay homage to the jewel-colored treasures that are perfectly aligned in glass cases.

I approach these cases and stand for a few moments surveying the beautiful chocolates, for they truly are extraordinary in appearance. Vibrant yellow, green, orange, and lavender cover what has become known as some of the finest chocolate in the country. A giddy feeling rises up inside me as I hear the words, "What would you like?"

The maestro emerges from the kitchen seen from behind a large window, and his appearance is equally surprising, because I'm expecting to see the white chef's jacket, maybe a laurel around his head as the crown prince of chocolate. But Christopher Elbow is wearing a Kansas City Royals T-shirt and blue jeans; he looks like Mr. Anybody-on-the-Street, and this chocolate-making rock star has an equally unassuming

Christopher Elbow. Courtesy of Deborah Reinhardt.

demeanor. He's just a nice guy from the Midwest making the best chocolate you may ever taste.

We sit on stools at a bar in his shop to discuss how a boy from Liberty, Mo., came to be a nationally acclaimed chocolatier.

Elbow's culinary career started in 1992, when he worked at a country club in Lincoln, Neb. After graduating from the University of Nebraska in 1996 with a Bachelor of Science degree in restaurant and business administration, he came to Kansas City to work at Shiraz restaurant. Three years later, he went to Las Vegas to help Chef Emeril Lagasse open his steakhouse at The Venetian, and then later helped open the Eiffel Tower Restaurant at Paris Resort and Casino with Chef Jean Joho.

He returned to Kansas City in 2000 to work briefly at Shiraz again and then moved on to the award-winning American Restaurant, where he worked as a pastry chef. It was here that Elbow discovered the dessert side of the business.

He would make chocolates to send out to guests at the end of their meal. Fascinated by how chocolate can be used as a medium to create something artistic – like a sculptor would use bronze or a painter watercolors – Elbow taught himself how to make beautiful things out of chocolate. Customers started to ask about the wonderful chocolate candy, and in 2003, Elbow took the next step. He fixed up space above Shiraz for his kitchen and made his artisanal chocolates for mail order and small wholesale business.

Elbow won Best of Show in 2004 at the Next Generation Chocolatier

Courtesy of Deborah Reinhardt.

national competition; two years later, he won Best Flavor for his Earl Grey ganache. He has been featured on Food Network and in Oprah Winfrey's magazine.

His retail shop in Kansas City opened in 2007, and later, he opened his chocolate boutique in San Francisco.

Elbow says he draws from his savory cooking experience to create the unusual flavor profiles for his chocolates. For example, one of the savory-with-sweet flavors features caramel infused with fresh rosemary enrobed in a dark chocolate shell that's beautifully molded and colored a vibrant green. Another features caramel blended with strawberries and aged balsamic vinegar. The soft caramel is so velvety and packed with intense flavors, it's pleasurable to simply let it melt on your tongue – if you're that disciplined.

"Every day, every batch we make, we pay attention to all the detail so they come out perfect," Elbow says. He says they never put out anything – even as a sample – that is not perfect. A batch may consist of 900 to 1,200 pieces, each enrobed by hand.

The blend of chocolate used to enrobe each piece is one of the most important details Elbow had to work out. Because of the more than 20 different flavors – including passion fruit, champagne, and Kansas City whiskey – Elbow says he had to make a chocolate to complement each piece. He made several trips to France and tested 30 to 40 different chocolate blends before he had the right one that would provide him with the correct balance. With each piece, one tastes chocolate, followed by the flavor in the center and then chocolate at the end. Each piece, each time. Remarkable.

And because his supplier works directly with farmers in countries like Madagascar, Elbow says he feels really good about using the chocolate. Locally sourced ingredients are used whenever possible, and needless to say, there's nothing artificial in any of his chocolates.

Elbow says there are about 16 core flavors that are offered year-round, and twice a year, he changes up flavors to match the seasons. Spring and summer see flavors that incorporate mint, lemon, basil, and berries. Fall and winter will bring pear, apple, and maple flavors to the table.

"The process (of coming up with flavors) never turns off in my brain," Elbow says. "It's instinctive now. The first thing I think of is: will this work with chocolate?"

Making his incredible chocolate is the easy part of his job, Elbow says. The challenge is always around managing the growth of the business.

"We're at a place where we're still organically growing," he says.

The necessity-is-the-mother-of-invention idea is what led to the opening of Elbow's artisanal ice cream shops, Glacé. During summer, the chocolate business slows down some, so he started to make ice cream using the same flavors as in his chocolates. It originally was sold at the chocolate shop, until he opened the first ice cream store in 2010.

But for many of his customers, chocolate is something that's enjoyed all the time.

"We have people that come in every day. I love seeing it consumed in this way. Europeans will buy bread and chocolate each day. They eat well and live well, and to me, that's really living."

Christopher Elbow Artisanal Chocolate
www.elbowchocolates.com

1819 McGee St.
Kansas City, MO 64108
(816) 842-1300
Store hours are 8 a.m. to 5 p.m.
Monday-Friday

Christopher Elbow Chocolates are available at many locations in the greater Kansas City area, including Better Cheddar shops in Country Club Plaza and Prairie Village, Kan., and at Cosentino's Markets. See the website for additional information.

Connect with Christopher Elbow Chocolates on Facebook, Pinterest or Twitter.

Tasty Tidbits

Crossroads District

What once was an urban area filled with vacant buildings has become a vibrant, eclectic arts district filled with galleries, shops, and restaurants. A great time to visit Crossroads District is during First Fridays. As the name implies, on the first Friday of each month from 7 to 9 p.m., businesses feature art and offer specials. Music can be found indoors and out.

Dining options are varied, including barbecue, Italian, Mexican, Thai, steaks, and more. The newer Kauffman Center for the Performing Arts is nearby, and if you want to hear traditional Kansas City jazz, the iconic Green Lady Lounge, 1809 Grand Blvd., is a great choice.

For more information, visit the Kansas City Convention and Visitors Association site, www.visitkc.com.

Courtesy of Visit KC.

Boulevard Brewing Company

Kansas City

Belgian beer and chocolate. It's a sure bet, like putting a few bucks on American Pharoah to win.

So it shouldn't be a surprise that a chocolate ale made by Boulevard Brewing Company's Brewmaster Steven Pauwels and Kansas City's famed chocolatier Christopher Elbow is wonderful. What might be surprising is how Boulevard's beer-drinking fans clamor for the chocolate brew.

Founded in 1989, Boulevard has become the largest specialty brewer in the Midwest. Since the debut of Boulevard's chocolate ale in February 2011, the brewing company has increased the amount it manufacturers each year; it now exceeds the other releases in the Smokestack or limited-release series. As soon as it appears on the shelves each February, it's gone.

Pauwels, who came to Boulevard from Belgium in 1990, says he has always had a good deal of respect for Elbow, and adds that he is underrated as one of the country's best chocolatiers.

Courtesy of Boulevard Brewing Company.

"And Chris is big time into beer, so it was easy to convince him to do a collaboration," Pauwels says. "He was very involved in the process to incorporate the flavor of chocolate into beer."

That process may seem unusual, but then specialty breweries often push the envelope. After the beer is made, Pauwels says, the cocoa nibs – pieces of roasted cacao beans – are placed in pantyhose and dunked into the beer. The nibs hang in the beer tanks for two weeks as the cocoa flavors are released.

The cocoa beans come from the Dominican Republic and are noted for having a robust aroma, which harmonizes well with the beer's malt. Other natural flavors, like vanilla and spices, give the beer its bittersweet finish. The spring seasonal beer is presented in dramatic 750-ml bottles and is also available locally on draught. It pairs well with Mexican food, Pauwels suggests.

Brewmaster Steven Pauwels. Courtesy of Boulevard Brewing Company.

In June 2015, Boulevard introduced its Aztec Chocolate Imperial Stout. For this beer, which receives inspiration from the ancient chocolate drink called *xocoatl*, Ceylon cinnamon is brewed into the Imperial Stout, which is then infused with the cocoa nibs, *pasilla negro,* and ancho chiles. Because the Imperial Stout is "a bigger beer," Pauwels says, more of the cocoa nibs are used, but the process of suspending them in the tanks is similar to making the chocolate ale. A rich caramel taste combines with the heat from the chiles for a full mouthfeel. Pauwels suggests pouring some of the stout over ice cream for dessert. Of course, simply enjoying a tulip glass of the brew after a meal is also acceptable. Aztec Chocolate Imperial Stout, another limited-series brew, is only available in the 750-ml bottles.

Pauwels is a big believer in collaborating with others in the culinary field to create something new and wonderful.

"That's the way to do it," he says. "We're all craftsmen trying to be very good at what we do. Together, we can be much stronger than doing something just by ourselves. There's great food and drink being produced now. It's a really good time to be in Missouri."

Boulevard Brewing Company
www.boulevard.com

2501 Southwest Blvd.
Kansas City, MO 64108
(816) 474-7095

Boulevard offers free 40-minute tours of their brewing facility at various times seven days a week. It's first-come, first-served; the weekend often fills up quickly. The tour ends in the Tasting Room to sample a variety of Boulevard beers. Or purchase a flight of four-ounce beers for $5 in the Tasting Room. There also are longer, specialized tours for smaller groups that go more in-depth that and are available by reservation and a fee of $20.

Boulevard distributes to 25 states. Smokestack Series beers are available in restaurants, bars and retail outlets. Visit the "beer finder" on the company website to see what's available near you.

Connect with Boulevard on Facebook, Twitter, YouTube or Flickr.
There's also an interesting beer blog on Boulevard's website.

Chip's Chocolate Factory

Kansas City

Crown Center in the heart of Kansas City is made for children. So much more than a shopping mall, Crown Center has an entertaining mix of kid-friendly shops, restaurants, and attractions scattered throughout three levels. One such place is Chip's Chocolate Factory.

For more than 30 years, Chip's Chocolate Factory has been part of Crown Center. Located on the second level, Chip's sells much more than delicious Kansas City Fudge® at this prime location; fun is a key component of what happens at the factory.

Okay, where are the Oompa-Loompas?

Chip's Chocolate Factory does have a bit of a Willy Wonka vibe to it. From the imaginative sign over the front entrance, which looks like chocolate dripping from metal gears, to the workers making candy in the window, customers can't help but be drawn inside.

Once in the shop, you feel like, well, a kid in a candy store, because sweet treats are everywhere. Candy apples bigger than your fist are covered in caramel, nuts, or candies and drizzled with white or milk

Courtesy of Deborah Reinhardt.

chocolate. Marshmallow and rice-cereal treats dipped in chocolate and decorated with candy sprinkles tempt you to pluck them from buckets. Bonbons, pecan or cashew clusters, a variety of chocolate barks, and turtles the size of the palm of your hand tease you from glass cases. In all, Chip's Chocolate Factory offers about 200 different confections.

And then there's the famous fudge. More than 40 flavors – such as Rocky Road, Strawberry Cheesecake, Birthday Cake, and Cotton Candy – are made fresh, by hand, in the shop.

Michael Herman is the president of KC Fudge, Inc. – and Chip's Chocolate Factory's own Willy Wonka. He says the company turns out up to 45,000 pounds of fudge every year. The top-selling flavors are Creamy Chocolate, Chocolate Walnut, Chocolate Pecan, Chocolate Pecan Turtle, Chocolate Peanut Butter, and Chocolate Mudslide. The company started in 1983, making just the Creamy Chocolate fudge.

Today, Herman says, there are two full-time confectioners who do four to six fudge-making demonstrations a day.

And it's a fascinating procedure to watch. Ingredients – sugar, whole milk, corn syrup and salt – are stirred together in a big copper until it reaches about 230 degrees. Chocolate is stirred in with a paddle, and when it's ready, the mixture is poured onto a marble table.

Then the real fun begins.

The confectioner continuously works the mixture, scraping, stirring and even flipping it into the air. When asked what the trickiest part of the process is, Herman says he can't give away trade secrets. "But I can tell you that making Kansas City Fudge® is not a process that you can set on autopilot," he says.

"We don't use preservatives, marshmallow cream or butter to give our product its trademark creaminess," he adds. "Each batch is different, and each flavor has

Courtesy of Deborah Reinhardt.

its own set of specific circumstances to watch and anticipate when making it. Basically, you've got to be on your toes for every batch."

While the process is as important as the recipe when it comes to making fudge, quality ingredients are important, too. Herman says he uses certified fair-trade chocolate imported from Switzerland. The company also does all it can to source ingredients from local suppliers.

However Herman makes the magic, he does it well. I tasted the Chocolate Peanut Butter (Herman's favorite flavor), as well as the Strawberry Cream. Just a small pinch of the Chocolate Peanut Butter has such a rich chocolate flavor with peanut butter in the background. The texture is creamy and the fudge melts on your tongue – when you can control yourself long enough to let it. The Strawberry Cream is a fresh pop of berry that tastes like a strawberry shortcake.

Courtesy of Deborah Reinhardt.

Herman says he's always looking for new ideas to offer something fresh to his customers.

"Being a small business that is closely held and family-run, our limits are our imagination and ability to put our ideas into something edible, sweet, aesthetically pleasing, and in demand," he says.

Like Willy Wonka, Herman is a very savvy businessman. He knows that, in the candy business, delicious confections have to be accompanied with great customer service. He's always trying to work better and smarter, and he says that's the best part of his job.

"If we're doing something – anything – then there's probably a good chance that we can do it better. I've said to customers many times over the years that while we strive to provide an exceptional product and topnotch customer service, that despite our greatest efforts, there will be times when we don't get it right.

"When that happens, I assume full and complete responsibility, and then use that as an opportunity to get it right, get it better, and get it great," he says.

And with that kind of dedication, you don't need Oompa-Loompas.

Chip's Chocolate Factory
www.kcfudge.com

2450 Grand Blvd.
Kansas City, MO 64108
(816) 421-0012

Store hours are 10 a.m. to 7 p.m. Monday-Saturday, Noon to 6 p.m. Sunday.

The fudge and other confections are available at the Crown Center location or can be ordered online and shipped anywhere in the United States.

Connect with Chip's Chocolate Factory on Facebook or Twitter.

Tasty Tidbits

Crown Center

One of the first mixed-use developments in the country, Crown Center welcomes approximately 5 million visitors a year. The 85-acre complex recently added SEA LIFE Aquarium and LEGOLAND® Discovery Center to its mix of kid-friendly attractions.

Visitors can also get creative at Kaleidoscope, which uses leftover material from Hallmark's manufacturing process for children's art projects. Creative performances are offered at the Coterie Theater, and the Crayola® Store Kansas City will bring out the artist in anyone. Next door, the Crayola® Cafe is the only one of its kind in the country.

Crown Center's district is also home to Kansas City's Union Station attraction, a wonderful development that houses a great science center, movie theater, and restaurants in the historical train station that dates to 1914. The Money Museum and the impressive National World War I Museum at Liberty Memorial are also nearby.

The center hosts events throughout the year, but during the winter holidays, a special magic enfolds the district. The city's Christmas tree is here and lit annually with great fanfare, and the Crown Center Ice Terrace has been a winter family tradition for more than 40 years.

For more information, visit www.crowncenter.com or call (816) 274-8444. Follow Crown Center on Twitter, Facebook, or YouTube.

Panache Chocolatier

Kansas City

Panache: lots of energy and style (Merriam-Webster Dictionary)

Country Club Plaza is Kansas City's stylish epicenter. This is prime real estate for residents and businesses and one of the most visited parts of the city. As the country's first shopping center, Country Club Plaza, which dates to the early 1920s, has seen a lot of change and growth, but Panache, a small chocolate boutique, has been a part of the Plaza for 36 years.

So when Julie and Derrick House, who were shopping for a business they could buy, had the chance to acquire Panache, the couple knew they couldn't mess with some traditions, such as the recipes for favorites like Choco Poppo (caramel popcorn drizzled with milk or dark chocolate).

Courtesy of Panche Chocolatier.

But, like a lady who has had the same hairstyle for many years, Panache needed a bit of a makeover.

"We were looking at every type of business, from A to Z, but we

Courtesy of Panche Chocolatier.

kept coming back to this," Julie House says. "We made a list of pros and cons and looked at what the business needed." Finally, they, along with business partners Joe and Erica Ismert, bought Panache.

Then the real fun began.

House said the business hadn't changed in almost 30 years. "Retail is about change and growth and keeping your products fresh." So the couple set out to rebrand the business, and they started with the space.

The store was "stripped back to just the studs", says House, whose background is in interior design. Then, as if touched by a fairy godmother, the shop was put back together in just 12 days. Workers, including the Houses, pulled long hours to get it all done. They reopened in in time for one of the Plaza's biggest annual events – the Art Fair – at the end of September.

"It was a *really* long weekend," House says with a wry smile, "but it was a great way to meet the other merchants and customers."

The new store looks as though it could be Greta Garbo's boudoir. It's glamorous and beautiful, but it doesn't shout at you. Light fixtures drip in crystal. Rich wood-and-tile flooring leads the way to crisp white displays of caramels, truffles and the ubiquitous Choco Poppo. There's a lot of white in the store, which creates the illusion of a bigger space. Cozy tables inside and out provide seating opportunities when ordering from the café menu, which includes hot and cold drinks, ice cream treats or fresh pastries, including pretty French macarons. Patrons also can order a few pieces of handmade chocolate to enjoy with a glass of wine. House says the majority of established customers love the store's new design.

But notice that what is inside the glass-topped display cases, artfully arranged on classic white serving dishes, is as beautiful as the shop itself. In addition to the customer favorites, House has already added 45 new items. Truffles are rolled by hand and dipped in rich Belgium chocolate.

House says she experiments with new flavors all the time. During my visit, lemon poppyseed and mango margarita truffles were available. Only a few dozen truffles of a particular flavor are made at a time, which allows for experimenting with different combinations, expanding selections, and making sure the chocolates are always at their peak of fresh flavor. It can be quite a process.

"Chocolate can be temperamental," House says. "It likes to play with you."

But chocolatiers must get the last word, as I hear workers in the kitchen pounding chocolate blocks into pieces to prepare for tempering.

Another customer favorite, the butter caramels, have a well-balanced taste of chocolate and velvety vanilla, and just the right amount of sea salt on top satisfies that salty-

Courtesy of Panche Chocolatier.

sweet craving. A box of about 15 caramels covered in milk or dark chocolate makes a wonderful hostess gift.

"I used to not like dark chocolate, but after tasting ours, I've changed," House says, adding that their chocolate is rich without having any bitter taste.

For the immediate future, in addition to making wonderful chocolates, plans for Panache include refining the online ordering process and upgrading the website. Expanding to additional locations is a long-term goal, but right now, the goal for Panache is simple.

"We're trying to make it a place where people can come in and enjoy our hospitality, a glass of wine, and a truffle."

You have to figure Garbo would approve.

Courtesy of Panche Chocolatier.

Panache Chocolatier
www.chocolatekc.com

418 Nichols Road
Kansas City, MO 64112
(816) 931-3191

Store hours are 8:30 a.m. to 7 p.m. Monday-Wednesday; 8:30 a.m. to 9 p.m. Thursday-Saturday; 10 a.m. to 5 p.m. Sunday.

Connect with Panache Chocolatier on Facebook.

Tasty Tidbits

Country Club Plaza

J.C. Nichols had a vision, and what a dream it was. Credited with starting Country Club Plaza, Nichols drew from his travels to Europe and the American Southwest, where he saw a development influenced by Spanish architecture. The Plaza opened in the early 1920s, and almost from its beginnings, it was clear this could be a special destination for Christmastime, when the very first string of holiday lights were hung in 1925.

Today, there are 15 blocks featuring more than 150 premier retail and restaurant options, and on the day after Thanksgiving, the Plaza literally glows. Spanish-style architecture, stunning fountains and outdoor artwork combine to make the Plaza more than a unique outdoor shopping center; it is Kansas City's prime gathering spot, for residents and visitors alike.

Chocolate and food fans can check out shops such as The Better Cheddar specialty food store, Cupcake A La Mode, IT'SUGAR candy store, Sur La Table or Williams-Sonoma. Sit down to enjoy chocolate at The Melting Pot (try the chocolate dessert fondue) or The Cheesecake Factory (Godiva chocolate cheesecake is classic).

For more information, visit the Kansas City Convention and Visitors Association site, www.visitkc.com.

Courtesy of Visit KC.

Southmoreland on the Plaza

Kansas City

It's said that when Russell and Clara Stover lived in Denver, Colo., neighbors on Detroit Street were intrigued by intoxicating aromas coming from Clara's kitchen. Turns out, she was making hand-dipped chocolates for Mrs. Stover's Bungalow Candies, and the scent of vanilla combining with chocolate, cream, and butter had the neighbors following their noses to her door.

Similarly, guests staying at Southmoreland Inn near Country Club Plaza in Kansas City may follow their noses to the open kitchen of innkeepers Nancy Miller and Mark Reichle because one never knows what delicious dish the couple may be cooking.

Miller and Reichle, both former human resources executives for Ford Motor Company, have owned the inn for 17 years, after purchasing it from the original innkeepers, Susan Moehl and Penni Johnson. But the house dates to 1913 and was a private residence until about 1990. Reichle says guests often return to the inn for the food, something he and Miller are passionate about. It's a large part of the hospitality they extend to guests, and it starts with wine and light appetizers in the early evening, hot beverages and sweets – including the to-die-for chocolate pixie cookies – and a full gourmet breakfast.

The kitchen seems to be the center of the inn, much like any home. Guests can watch the innkeeper baking cookies for the evening or chocolate zucchini bread to include with breakfast the next day. The chocolate bread, Miller says, is usually baked once a week, it's that popular.

Over the years, the couple has gathered recipes that guests seem to like best and, in 2007, published the Southmoreland cookbook, *Tried & True* ($19.95). They also offer recipes on the blog that's part of their website. Miller and Reichle understand that details matter a great deal in the hospitality business, and they do not miss a single one.

For example, if you're lucky enough to score the chocolate Belgian waffles for breakfast, you will have chocolate mint buttercream as an accompaniment (if you don't just eat it by the spoonful, it's that good).

Special occasions often bring guests to a B&B, and Southmoreland's owners know how to help guests celebrate. It's possible to add extras to a room reservation, such as flowers, chocolate-covered strawberries or, if you really want to make an impression, the Kansas City Sweet Treats package. Miller says since moving to Kansas City, they have discovered wonderful culinary delights, and for this package, they've put together frosted shortbread cookies from McClain's Bakery, chocolate-covered almonds

Chocolate Belgian Waffles. Courtesy of Deborah Reinhardt.

from Andrés, some Christopher Elbow chocolates, and a sample from The Better Cheddar.

The Russell and Clara Stover room is often reserved by guests seeking a romantic getaway. Miller says those in the Stover room receive a box of Stover chocolates as part of the turndown service (all guests receive a piece of chocolate in the evenings).

All rooms have a private bath, but there's a two-person whirlpool tub in the Stover room, which is decorated as though it were Mrs. Stover's original bungalow. Pastel colors create the sweet palette. Roses decorate the room's wallpaper, and pink carpet almost makes one believe she's walking on rose petals. A large brass bed and antiques complete the romantic ambiance.

Courtesy of Deborah Reinhardt.

The inn has 12 guest rooms, each named for a famous Kansas Citian, plus a carriage-house suite that overlooks the beautiful courtyard. It is in this courtyard that Miller and Reichle offer what they call "Barbecue Breakfast" – which makes sense in Kansas City – from mid-April to mid-October. On my visit, Reichle was grilling molasses-brined pork chops and peaches to accompany croissant French toast in maple pecan sauce. Meanwhile, Miller brings guests mango-strawberry smoothies and whatever additional beverage they desire (coffee, tea or juice). While waiting to turn the pork chops on the beautiful stone grill, Reichle chats with some of the guests about their plans for the day. And within walking distance, there's plenty for guests to do, such as visit three art museums or explore the Plaza.

But when you're staying in such a welcoming inn, there's no rush to get going.

Southmoreland on the Plaza
www.southmoreland.com

116 E. 46th St.
Kansas City, MO 64112
(816) 531-7979

Connect with Southmoreland on Facebook and Twitter.

Chase Candy Company

St. Joseph

Barry Yantis gets to the office each work day between 4:30 and 5 a.m., but as CEO of the Chase Candy Company in St. Joseph, Mo., he doesn't mind the early hours.

"Candymakers start early," he says. "I've made every kind of candy here. Two days after starting the job, I was spreading peanut brittle."

Chase Candy, which dates to 1876, makes one of the oldest candy bars in the country – Cherry Mash. In fact, more than 70,000 bars are turned out each day in the factory on the east end of town. Yantis says it remains America's favorite cherry-flavored candy bar.

For the uninitiated, Cherry Mash isn't shaped in a bar; it's round, with a fondant center flavored with maraschino cherries and covered in a compound chocolate and crushed-peanut coating.

The candy was formulated around 1918 by George Washington Chase, the St. Joseph doctor who made candy to supplement his income. He went on to open Chase Candy. The business prospered, and in the early 1920s, Chase had a four-story factory in downtown St. Joseph,

Courtesy of the Chase Candy Company.

with the family's third generation, Charles, joining the business. By 1926, Chase had made more than 500 different candies – although not all would go on to be successful.

The F.S. Yantis Company purchased Chase in 1944; the family is the present owner of Chase Candy Company.

When asked why the Chase family chose cherry to make a candy bar, Yantis says, "I really don't know. It was so long ago, but it's the survivor."

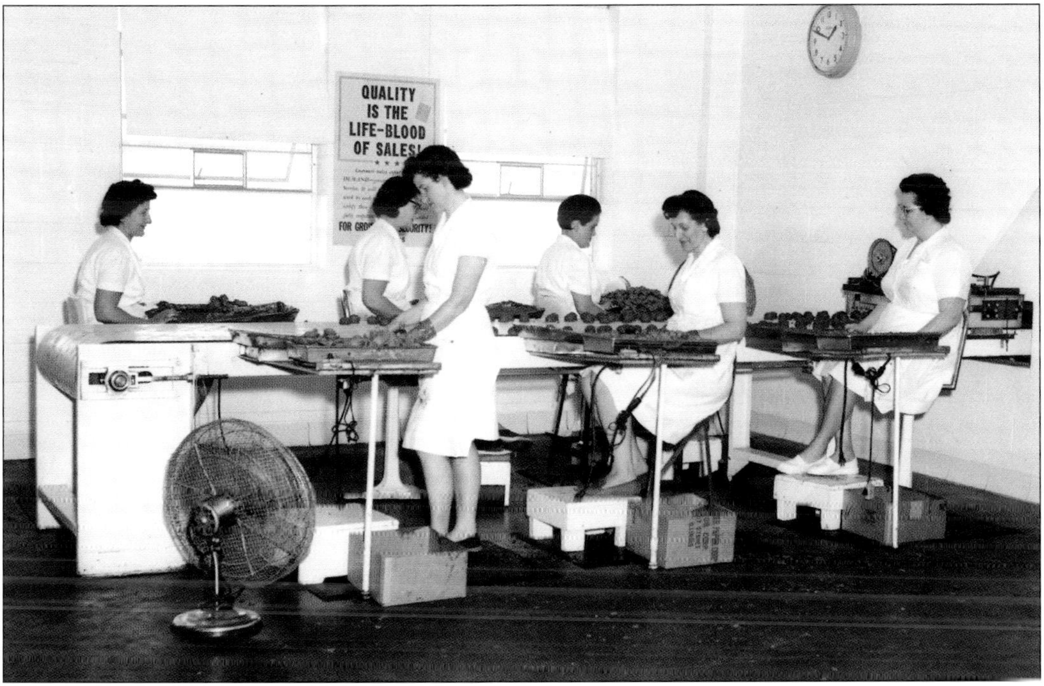

The ladies hand dipped the Cherry Mash with an ice cream scoop, being done this way when Barry started in 1974. Courtesy of the Chase Candy Company.

In its familiar red-and-white striped package with the little "Candy Cop" on the side, Cherry Mash is readily found in Midwestern grocery stores, convenience store, and specialty candy shops, as well as nationwide Hobby Lobby stores.

Courtesy of the Chase Candy Company.

The iconic Candy Cop dates to the early 1930s. During the Great Depression, Ernest Chase had a friend in the ad business in Chicago. Times being what they were, Chase wanted to give his friend a little work. He asked him to develop a corporate mascot for Cherry Mash. While early versions seem to resemble the popular Kewpie dolls, the Candy Cop endures.

And so has the company.

In the 1950s, Chase Candy, after acquiring Bunte Brothers Candy Company, left St. Joseph for Chicago, and the company was known as Bunte-Chase. However, by 1961, the Chicago plant closed and Chase returned to St. Joseph. Later, Chase purchased the Poe Candy Company, which was known for its coconut and peanut candies that were cooked in copper kettles.

Yantis says the addition of other candies put the squeeze on the old factory. "We were running out of space," he says.

In 2005, Chase Candy opened its present factory, designed to accommodate their candy-making business. In addition to Cherry Mash, product made at the location includes peanut brittle, the chewier peanut squares and peanut-coconut Peco Flake, chocolate peanut clusters, coconut bonbons, and haystacks.

Yantis realizes his company remains a smaller business in the confectioners' arena. His biggest challenge is the constant battle for shelf space to sell his product.

"We're up against corporations like Hershey and Nestle," Yantis says. "They have a lot of promotional money. Of course, we can't compete with that."

But Yantis has something much more valuable in his marketing arsenal – a fiercely loyal customer base. It is not a stretch to say people love Cherry Mash. Yantis has drawers of letters and poems from people who write to thank him for the candy – and the many memories associated with it.

Colorado-based songwriter and performer, Jim Salestrom, wrote a song to express his feelings for the candy. As a boy growing up in Kearney, Neb., Salestrom knows all about Cherry Mash.

It all reminds Yantis of the importance of keeping his customers happy.

"It's important to make the candy perfect," he says. "There are real people out there buying it and enjoying Cherry Mash. When I meet people and tell them I make Cherry Mash, every one of them has a story about Cherry Mash. It's amazing."

Chase Candy Company
www.cherrymash.com

1307 S. 59th St.
St. Joseph, MO 64507
(800) 786-1625

There are no tours of the factory, but candy is available for purchase during regular business hours Monday through Friday. The website also offers a search option to find Cherry Mash in a retail location near you.

Connect with Chase Candy Company on Facebook, Twitter or YouTube.

TASTY TIDBITS

St. Joseph, Mo.

It's fitting that St. Joseph is one of the main stops along The Way of American Genius, Missouri Highway 36. As the birthplace of the Pony Express, the site of the Walter Cronkite Memorial at Missouri Western State University and a hub of 19th-century wealth and industry, St. Joseph has seen entrepreneurialism at its best.

A rich history stemming from connections to Jesse James, the Civil War and Lewis and Clark is here to explore. You may be surprised to see the outstanding examples of historical architecture throughout the city, which was an important spot for 19th-century commerce and trade. Explore the city's history at the Wyeth-Tootle Mansion, one of several wonderful museums in town. Visit Mount Mora Cemetery, one of the state's oldest, during October and experience a living history walking tour called "Voices of the Past."

Shop for antiques, gifts, clothing, home decor and much more in St. Joseph. Get your cowboy or cowgirl on with a visit to the Stetson hat outlet or St. Joe Boot Co. Twelve annual festivals provide additional reasons to visit.

Plan your trip by contacting the St. Joseph Convention and Visitors Bureau at (800) 785-0360 or www.StJoMO.com. To learn more about the Way of American Genius, visit www.AmericanGeniusHighway.com.

These photos depict the Pony Express history at St. Joseph. The young man on horseback is identified as Johnny Fry, a Pony Express re-enactor. The three women on horseback are in front of the historical Patee House Museum, a national landmark. Photos courtesy of Missouri Division of Tourism.

Chocolaterie Stam

Hannibal

Mary Glenn and Tony Bowman have experienced two perfect matches in their lives.

High-school sweethearts, the Hannibal, Mo., couple will have been married 50 years in 2016. Like most couples who can boast that kind of longevity in their relationship, The Bowmans no doubt have learned to take what life brings.

Which brings us to the second perfect match. Chocolate and one adventurous couple. And like many perfect matches, this one happened quite by chance.

In 2011, the couple visited Rochester, Minn., for medical appointments at the Mayo Clinic. While walking through a nearby mall, they noticed what they thought was an ice cream store, so they went in for a much-deserved treat.

The proprietor explained he sold gelato and fine, European-style chocolates. One taste and Mary Glenn was hatching a plan – before the chocolate had even melted on her tongue.

"I told Tony we had to get this into Hannibal somehow," she says.

Mary Glenn and Tony had just discovered Chocolaterie Stam, a chocolate company from Amsterdam, and the couple was on their way to becoming Missouri's only Stam franchise.

Although Mary Glenn had retired in 2009, after 25 years as a travel agent, and was not sure

Courtesy of Missouri Division of Tourism.

what to do with all of her free time, she said starting a business wasn't a part of her retirement plans. "I didn't know anything about chocolate, other than I liked it," Mary Glenn said.

Jacob Stam liked chocolate, too.

In 1817, the Stams had a bakery in Holland just north of Amsterdam. People soon recognized the business for its quality pastries and chocolates, often recommending to the family that they focus exclusively on chocolate. By 1913, Jacob Stam made that decision and opened Chocolaterie Stam, and by the

1930s, his children – sons Frits, Wim, and Jaap, as well as daughter, Fredi – joined Jacob in the business.

Frits became quite successful in his development of Stam chocolates, and it was his youngest son, Ton, who led the chocolate company across the ocean to America in 1997. His nephew, Erik, is the master chocolatier for the company today, which has its U.S. headquarters in Des Moines, Iowa. There are Stam franchises in six states within the Midwest.

Mary Glenn said she had to sell Ton Stam on the idea of locating a chocolaterie in Hannibal. She had to convince him the town was big enough to support a Stam store, so she explained Hannibal's draw for tourists. He asked her why people come to Hannibal.

Um, ever heard of Mark Twain?

"He said, 'Who?'" Mary Glenn recalls.

But she was able to make her case, and on Sept. 7, 2011, Chocolaterie Stam opened on Main Street.

"Guess I wasn't ready to retire," Mary Glenn says. "I'm here pretty much every day, except weekends."

And Ton has since become a fan of Mark Twain's books.

Before the store opened, however, Mary Glenn traveled to Iowa to learn about Stam's Dutch chocolate techniques. It was a crash course in chocolate-making, but she said it was a lot of fun.

"I've never been anywhere where it smelled any better," she says.

She also noted the process hasn't changed too much in 100 years. The artistic candy molds from 1913 are still used. Stam's trademark bonbons, enrobed in milk and dark Belgian chocolate, come in 40 flavors. Mary Glenn said one of their best-selling bonbons is forest berry cream, molded chocolate shaped into a tiny accordion and filled with cream and a layer of berry preserves. The sea salt caramels are also quite popular. All of her candy is made in Iowa, not on-site.

Courtesy of Missouri Division of Tourism.

"It's got a very European flavor to it. We have customers come in and they know exactly what they want, and we better not be out of it," she says with a chuckle. Some of her regular customers drive 30 miles from Quincy, Ill., for their favorite box of bonbons.

Tourists often seem surprised to find a shop like Stam in Hannibal, but curiosity draws them in. Mary Glenn said they may purchase a few bonbons, but before leaving town, it's not unusual to see them return to purchase a box to take home as a gift.

Other candies include wine gummies and licorice. Stam also sells its own blend of coffee, available to sip at the store or in whole-bean form to take home. House-made Italian gelato – as many as 200 different flavors, including many chocolate varieties – is also sold. A selection of Missouri-made wines are also available in the shop for those who want to enjoy a local vintage with fine chocolate.

"We've got something for everybody," Mary Glenn said.

And Mary Glenn and her husband like being in the people-pleasing business. The best part of her job, she said, is interacting with her customers. Mary Glenn's father and grandfather had a store in downtown Hannibal, too; it would seem shopkeeping is in her blood.

"People always come in with a smile on their face. It's been a fun four years," she said.

Chocolaterie Stam
www.stamchocolate.com

103 N. Main St.
Hannibal, MO 63401
(573) 221-0460

Hours are 10 a.m. to 6 p.m. Monday–Thursday; 10 a.m. to 9 p.m. Friday and Saturday; noon to 5 p.m. Sunday.

Connect with Chocolaterie Stam on Facebook.

Hannibal, Mo.

Fans of American author and humorist Samuel Clemens (Mark Twain) come from all over the world to see his hometown. Clemens, born in tiny Florida, Mo., moved to Hannibal with his family when he was 4 years old; he lived here until age 17, when he left home to make his mark on the world.

Most visitors will see the Mark Twain Boyhood Home and Museum in Hannibal, but there's certainly many other Twain-related sites and activities. Located on the Mississippi River, it's common to see the American Queen steamboat or smaller sightseeing riverboats docked here. A mix of shops and art galleries provide a nice divergence from the river and Twain history that surrounds Hannibal.

Dining options range from diners to nice restaurants. Chocolate lovers will want to try the Godiva chocolate cake for dessert at LaBinnah Bistro. Honest, stick-to-your-ribs Midwest comfort food is plentiful at Mark Twain Dinette, which has been part of Hannibal since 1942. The breaded pork tenderloin sandwich is as big as the plate; the loose ground-beef Maid-Rite sandwich is another popular choice for lunch or dinner. Save room for the Mississippi Mud Pie (a chocolate brownie served with ice cream, hot fudge, and whipped cream and topped with a cherry) or a float made with ice cream and the Dinette's homemade root beer.

Overnight options include a selection of chain motels plus some very nice B&Bs. If you want to stay where Twain slept, the beautiful Garth Woodside Mansion is your best option. There are several cottages nestled on the estate, and romance and gourmet-food packages include chocolate treats. Twain also visited Rockcliffe Mansion around the turn of the century, entertaining Hannibal society with his witty stories. The mansion is open for tours and also offers B&B accommodations.

Between the attractions and a wealth of festivals in Hannibal, you won't get bored. Signature events include the July 4 fun that is Tom Sawyer Days, as well as the Autumn Folklife Festival in October. Celebrate Twain's birthday here on Nov. 30, or come back in March for the Chocolate Extravaganza, in which two dozen downtown merchants offer chocolate-related treats and activities.

For more information, contact the Hannibal Convention and Visitors Bureau at (573) 221-2477 or visit www.visithannibal.com.

Bankhead Chocolates

Bowling Green

President Thomas Jefferson sent out the Lewis and Clark Expedition in 1804. Most of us were introduced to this story in grade school. We learned how Jefferson's act opened up the American West following the Louisiana Purchase. The Corps of Discovery, which left on their odyssey from Missouri, played a huge part in shaping America.

It's a fascinating historical coincidence that more than 100 years later, one of Jefferson's ancestors, in his own quest, stamped Bowling Green, Mo., with a sweet legacy of fine chocolates.

In 1919, Thomas Jefferson Bankhead, the president's great-grandson, started a chocolate shop as a spinoff from his successful restaurant in Bowling Green. Through the years, Bankhead Chocolates was passed to several owners, until 30 years ago, when Mary Orf bought the business. Her daughter, Laura Portwood, owned the shop until about two years ago, when the third generation, April Moore, became the sole owner. Moore used to help her grandmother Mary by packaging product and then learned how to hand-dip chocolates when her mother, Laura, owned the shop.

Genealogy is one of the tourism draws for Bowling Green, what with its 150 historical cemeteries and the Pike County Genealogical Society and Museum. But travelers exploring this quadrant of northeast Missouri also stop to see the hand-dipped chocolates being made at Bankhead.

They find that not too much has changed since 1919; the candies still are made in large copper kettles, cooled on marble tabletops, then cut and dipped by hand. It apparently is a recipe for quality candy sought after by a growing number of customers.

On her first day as full-time marketing director for Bankhead, Amy Haislet says the summer – usually a slower season for chocolate-makers – has been booming.

"We've never had this amount of business in the past as we've had this summer," she says. "That's a great problem to have."

Part of the draw, no doubt, is attributed to the growing popularity of Bankhead's summer bistro. The bistro's menu includes its popular house salad plus an assortment of sandwiches, including homemade chicken salad, and desserts. The scrumptious chocolate-covered strawberry pie is popular. The bistro closes in October.

Traditionally, the busy season for chocolate-makers gets going in late September or early October. That's when Bankhead will roll out their caramel apples. For Valentine's Day, the chocolate-covered strawberries practically fly out the door, although Haislet says the berries are available when fresh and in season during other times of the year.

Using locally sourced ingredients is important to Bankhead's process, and the company purchases these when supply meets demand. The chocolate used to make their candy is sourced from the United States, Haislet says.

Bankhead's signature candy is the Chocolate Drop Turtle, a square carmel with pecans topped with a chocolate drop. Haislet says it's her favorite. Moore's favorite Bankhead candy is the Sugar Cookie Truffle, a smooth white ganache that's flavored like a sugar cookie and dipped in white chocolate then topped with sprinkles. The different chocolate creams and nut clusters also sell well,

Haislet says. Other items available at Bankhead include molasses puffs, assorted chocolate creams, and chocolate-dipped orange peels.

In addition to the hand-dipped chocolates, Bankhead sells a variety of goodies from the nearby Amish farming community located off rural Highways Y and M. A selection of Amish-made popcorn, jellies and jams are sold at Bankhead. And, while it's not made on-site, Bankhead also offers taffy, hard candy sticks and similar old-fashioned sweets.

According to Moore, the biggest challenge for her business is judging the amount of candies for the different seasons, as well as tracking and planning for what will be popular with customers.

Plans for the future include expanding wholesale opportunities, as well as increasing the number of community arts and crafts shows and regional festivals that showcase Bankhead Chocolates.

Discovering wonderful chocolate is an adventure most of us would be more than willing to do.

Bankhead Chocolates

810 Business Highway 61
Bowling Green, MO 63334
(573) 324-2312

Hours during mid-September through early April are 9 a.m. to 5 p.m. Monday–Friday; 9 a.m. to 2 p.m. on Saturday; closed on Sunday. Call ahead for hours during other seasons.

Connect with Bankhead Chocolates on Facebook

Tasty Tidbits

Bowling Green, Mo.

Bowling Green is a perfect day trip from St. Louis, which is about an hour south on U.S. Highway 61. In addition to the nearby Amish shops, Bowling Green has a selection of antique stores for browsing; who knows, you might uncover treasure. Or pack a cooler in the car and head to Woods Smoked Meats, another family-owned business in town. Bring home some of Woods' award-winning ham, bacon, smoked poultry and bratwurst.

Between Bowling Green and Louisiana, Mo., off state Route UU, is the Saint Louis University Lay Center for the Arts and Sculpture Park. Truly a hidden gem, the 350-acre park was once the farm of John McElwee, a Revolutionary War hero, and his wife, Rhonda Black.

More history can be discovered by visiting the Champ Clark House, former home of Congressman Clark, who served as Speaker of the House from 1911-19. The home is a National Historic Landmark and regional museum.

Feed your sense of adventure by driving 30 minutes north to Hannibal, or cut across U.S. Highway 54 and head north to the river town of Louisiana or south to Clarksville, both located on state Route 79. The corridor of Route 79 between Clarksville and Hannibal is known as 50 Miles of Art, and travelers can find wonderful artisan and artist shops and galleries along the way. Studio tours are offered in March and November each year, with a smattering of other events hitting at different times of the year.

Summertime boating and fishing is found at Mark Twain Lake, about 30 minutes northwest of Bowling Green. Winter is popular for eagle-watching along the Mississippi River.

For more information, contact the Bowling Green Convention and Visitors Bureau at (573) 470-1196 or www.VisitBowlingGreenMOcom.

Sweet on These Stops...

When you're exploring places in Northern Missouri, you'll be sweet on these chocolate destinations, too.

Kansas City, Mo.

Russell Stover Candies, www.russellstover.com

Russell and Clara Stover began a candy business in their Denver, Colo., home, later opening a factory in town. A candy factory in Kansas City, Mo., in 1925 and a third factory began production in Lincoln, Neb., in 1942. By 1960, Louis Ward purchased the company, and in 2014 Lindt & Sprungli purchased Russell Stover Candies from the Ward family. The largest producer of boxed chocolates in the United States, Russell Stover's corporate headquarters are in Kansas City. Its stores are scattered in 17 states, including Missouri. Find Russell Stover shops in Bethany, Blue Springs, Boonville, Harrisonville, Lebanon, Ozark, Sedalia and St. Louis.

Smithville, Mo.

Nellie's Sweet Shoppe, www.nelliessweetshoppe.com

It's a bittersweet story as to how this little chocolate shop located about 20 miles north of Kansas City, Mo., came to be.

Janelle "Nellie" Tebbs lost a battle with malignant melanoma in early 2007. That summer, her sister, Ronna Mack, and parents, Harley and Jackie Morlock, saw a vacant red-and-white storefront in downtown Smithville that had recently been vacated. They discussed that it looked like it should be a candy store. With the support of family and friends, on Oct. 4, 2007, the family opened Nellie's Sweet Shoppe in honor of Janelle.

Visit the store for "sponge" candy (also called molasses puffs), haystacks, chocolate melt-away mints, nut clusters, truffles and peanut butter cups. There's also a variety of nostalgic candy, as well as fudge and ice cream.

A small corner of the store is dedicated to educate visitors about melanoma prevention, and some of the store's proceeds goes to fight this most serious type of skin cancer.

The shop's tagline reads, "take time to enjoy each day" and reminds all of us to appreciate what we have and to enjoy life's pleasures. Nellie's Sweet Shoppe is located at 115 E. Main, and is closed Sundays. For hours or more information, call (816) 873-3663.

Central Missouri

The heart of Missouri is home to the tallest man-made national monument, a vibrant college town, historical smaller cities, and a water playground. Chocolate lovers will find everything in this part of Missouri, from award-winning gourmet chocolates – including some made from hand-selected cocoa beans – to fabulous homemade fudge.

St. Louis

From a sleek west St. Louis County chocolate boutique to a landmark building on the north side that's more than a century old, the St. Louis chocolate story is as rich as a piece of, well, fine chocolate.

Noted for beer and baseball, St. Louis' chocolatiers are quietly doing their own thing, and doing it with wonderful taste and flair. Rick Jordan, a nationally recognized chocolatier, makes unusual chocolate creations almost too beautiful to eat. Spunky Sheila Kleinschmidt proves girls just want to have fun while making and eating artisan chocolate. The Abel family is building a sweet empire that spans the country, while the Karandzieff clan is content as an important anchor within its neighborhood, feeding hungry patrons tasty lunches and heavenly hash. Other chocolate businesses have similarly interesting stories to tell and confections to enjoy.

Some of the city's chocolate traditions can be traced to 1904, the year of the Louisiana Purchase Exposition (World's Fair) in St. Louis. Greek immigrant John L. Mavrakos settled in St. Louis that year, and soon opened a candy and ice cream shop at Vandeventer Avenue and Olive Street. In 1913, John and his wife, Madeline, launched what would become one of the city's beloved brands, Mavrakos Candy Company. During the company's peak years in the 1950s, Mavrakos had more than 15 retail stores in the area. The well-known recipes now are made and marketed through the Chocolate Chocolate Chocolate Company.

Did you know the sweet tradition for sweet dreams – leaving a chocolate on a pillow – was born in St. Louis in the 1950s? While staying at the Roberts Mayfair Hotel, actor Cary Grant left a trail of chocolates from the living room to his bedroom to woo lady visitors. The hotel was so impressed with his creative use of candy, housekeepers were told to put a chocolate on each guest's pillow at night. Known today as the Magnolia Hotel, Kristin Yantis, public relations spokesperson, said guests today are given a piece of locally made Bissinger's chocolate at bedtime for a sweet way to cap off their day.

Columbia

Home to the storied University of Missouri-Columbia, this city is growing a reputation for fine food and a vibrant fine arts scene.

Alan "Patric" McClure is the man behind Patric Chocolate, a craft chocolate company in Columbia, Mo. McClure is one of only three "bean-to-bar" chocolate makers in Missouri; the others are Askinosie Chocolate in Springfield, Mo., and Rick Jordan in St. Louis.

If you want to send a memorable gift to a student or favorite "Mizzou" fan, then you have to visit The Candy Factory in Columbia, the city's candy store since

1974, for its Mizzou Gift Basket that features chocolate-covered espresso beans, a chocolate graham cracker treat decorated with a tiger face, and more.

Hermann

One of the state's viticultural areas, Hermann wineries are extremely popular. Located in the heart of this small town is Ricky's Chocolate Box, a family business that makes chocolate truffles, clusters, and caramels, which pair nicely with some of the locally made wines. Stop by for chocolate-covered strawberries before heading to your favorite winery to add a special touch to your tasting experience.

Lake of the Ozarks

This water playground has been a favorite vacation destination in Missouri for more than 60 years. Many families have visited the lake for decades, making a stop at the historical and funky Bagnell Dam Strip. And what lake vacation doesn't call for some sweet homemade fudge? Happily, Grandma's Candy Kitchen has just the ticket.

Visit the quaint shop on the Strip and sample a flavor or two before picking your favorite. Be warned: the sea salt caramel fudge is pretty hard to turn down.

St. Charles

Travelers love the St. Charles area for its history and natural beauty. Another of the state's viticultural regions, the lush, rolling hills are dotted with wineries. Katy Trail State Park, a rails-to-trail project that celebrated 25 years in 2015, offers hikers and bikers a chance to enjoy the outdoors amid beautiful landscapes.

Historical Main Street in St. Charles is home to Riverside Sweets, a quaint candy shop/ice cream parlor. In the nearby suburb of Cottleville, VB Chocolate Bar is a wonderful getaway offering chocolate, cocktails, ice cream, and inviting indoor and outdoor spaces for conversation.

Central Missouri gives an accurate snapshot of the diversity of its chocolate destinations; there's a little something sweet for everyone to enjoy here, so let's get started.

Bissinger's Chocolates

St. Louis

Resembling a streetscape from Paris, the sidewalk boasts a fine sheen from a recent rain. Pedestrians pass up and down the pavement that is lined with boutiques, cafés and trees. The St. Louis neighborhood known as the Central West End is oh, so stylish, a pleasant mix of old money and well-to-do urban professionals with just enough grit to keep it from getting too stodgy. People live and visit here because they love the atmosphere, and I count myself among them.

As the name implies, the Central West End (CWE to locals) is on the western cusp of the St. Louis City limits and just about next door to Clayton, the St. Louis County government and business center. Location, location, location.

And the location I have my eye on is one of the CWE's anchors, Bissinger's. Long noted for fine handcrafted European chocolates, its European Confectionary and Cafe at 32 Maryland Plaza is a welcome respite on this rainy afternoon.

I order one raspberry and one chocolate French macaron – inspired by an 18th-century French recipe – and a cafe au lait, take it to a small table, and open a book. I feel like I've just crossed the Atlantic Ocean.

This European aura is part of Bissinger's staying power in a city that's nurturing and supporting a growing number of chocolatiers. With a history that stretches to King Louis XIV, who granted the Bissinger family a title of "Confiseur Imperial" (royal candy maker), and spokespeople that have included actress Lauren Bacall,

I almost want to lift my pinky finger when taking a bite out of a chocolate-dipped apricot.

Nods to Bissinger's chocolates from sources like Food Network to *Wine Spectator* magazine to Oprah (yes, *that* Oprah) are gathered as its vanilla caramels are gathered into pretty boxes. In 2014, the company was awarded a "sofi" (Specialty Outstanding Food Innovation) for its apple ghost chili salt caramel. Baby, that's a mouthful.

Bissinger's came to St. Louis in 1927 by way of Ohio. The original store was on McPherson Avenue in the CWE until 2008, when the confectionary-café opened. There also is a retail location in Plaza Frontenac – a very upscale shopping mall – and the company's newest location is not far from the Mississippi River in downtown St. Louis. The 1910 building was once occupied by the Missouri Kansas Texas Railroad, and Bissinger's bought the property in 2013, spent $11 million in renovations, and

Courtesy of Deborah Reinhardt.

encircled it with an electric security gate (it is located in a blighted industrial area of downtown, but the city hopes to develop this section of the riverfront). The production facility, administration offices, and a special event space are located in the building. Factory tours are available by appointment.

Having finished my afternoon repast, I gather my things to make my way to the nearby Saint Louis Art Museum, one of the city's best rainy day destinations.

Courtesy of Deborah Reinhardt.

But first, one more decision has to be made. Do I take home the pecan nut balls, beloved by Stanley Marcus (of Neiman-Marcus fame), go with the can't-miss caramels, or compromise with a taste of both in the bear claws that boast chunky pecans, caramel and chocolate?

Variety is the spice of life, so I choose a few of each. City living agrees with me.

Bissinger's Chocolates
www.bissingers.com

32 Maryland Plaza
St. Louis, MO, 63108
(314) 367-7750
Store hours fluctuate. Opens at 10. a.m. most days, and at noon Sunday. Advisable to call before traveling.

97 Plaza Frontenac
St. Louis, MO, 63131
(314) 432-1329
Store hours are Monday–Friday, 10 a.m. to 8 p.m.; Saturday, 10 a.m. to 7 p.m.; Sunday, noon to 6 p.m.

Chocolate factory tours
1600 N. Broadway
St. Louis, MO, 63102
(314) 615-2400
Tours reserved by appointment only at 10 a.m. on Monday, Wednesday or Friday.

Connect with Bissinger's chocolates on Facebook, Twitter, Pinterest, Instagram, and YouTube.

Tasty Tidbits

Forest Park

The urban oasis that's also St. Louis' cultural center is just a few minutes from Bissinger's store on Maryland Plaza. The 1,371-acre park is larger than New York's Central Park. Dedicated in 1876, the park hosted the Louisiana Purchase Expedition (World's Fair) in 1904, and a couple of the structures remain today, including the Saint Louis Art Museum. Cass Gilbert designed the Palace of Fine Arts for the World's Fair and it remained as the city's museum. A modern East Wing opened in 2013.

Four other cultural institutions call Forest Park home: the Saint Louis Zoo, Missouri History Museum, St. Louis Science Center, and The Muny (outdoor theater open during summer). For more information, visit the St. Louis Convention & Visitors Commission site, www.explorestlouis.com.

Right: A statue of St. Louis' namesake, King Louis IX of France, proudly stands in front of the Saint Louis Art Museum in beautiful Forest Park. Courtesy of Missouri Division of Tourism.

Below: Paddleboats ply the Grand Basin in front of Art Hill and the Saint Louis Art Museum in Forest Park. Courtesy of Missouri Division of Tourism.

Chocolate Chocolate Chocolate Company

St. Louis

If the name doesn't tell you what's going on at the Chocolate Chocolate Chocolate Company's factory and store, the aromas that greet you at the front door certainly will. Nestled among several warehouses in an industrial part of The Hill, a St. Louis neighborhood known for its Italian groceries and restaurants, the location may look plain, but once inside, chocolate lovers will not only learn about candy making and a bit of local history, they will taste some of the finest candy available anywhere.

With 8 stores in Missouri and Illinois, and a brisk wholesale business that boasts a recent 39-percent increase, owner Dan Abel Sr. and his family have built a sweet empire in the Gateway City, but not at the cost of quality, and not without a healthy pinch of tradition.

Fresh, top-shelf ingredients – including cocoa and cane sugar that's Fair Trade Certified – are used in all their artisan chocolates. Dan C. Abel Jr. – one of three adult children who are part of the business – gave me a tour of the 30,000-square-foot factory and explained how the magic is made, as well as the family's candy-making history.

Courtesy of Chocolate Chocolate Chocolate Company.

Abel's father met the daughter of a Greek chocolatier while in college in Ohio. He started working as a college sophomore for the Yum Yum Tree, and eventually worked his way to the vice president's job. He also met Rosalie, whom he would later marry, at college; she was from St. Louis, too.

Missing their hometown, Dan (the father) and Rosalie set up a franchised Yum Yum Tree in St. Louis on Chippewa Street in 1981. When the Yum Yum Tree's founder passed away, the Abels purchased the business. The name was changed to Chocolate Chocolate Chocolate Company because by then, the couple had their third child. By 2002, the company had store franchises in full swing.

In 2009, they relaunched the Mavrakos chocolate brand, once extremely popular in St. Louis. The Mavrakos Candy Company story also is interesting. Greek immigrant John L. Mavrakos settled in St. Louis in 1904 and soon opened a candy and ice cream shop at Vandeventer Avenue and Olive Street. In 1913, he and his wife, Madeline, started the Mavrakos Candy Company and over many years, the business soared, reaching a peak in the 1950s, when the family had 16 retail stores in St. Louis and a thriving catalog business. Customers loved the signature molasses puffs, coconut crescents, "heavenly hash," and "pecan burrs."

But the Mavrakos story ended in 1984, when the company sold to Archibald Candy, based in Chicago. Archibald was the company behind the Fannie May brand. Archibald closed its doors in 2004.

Luckily, the Mavrakos family's recipe book was given to Dan Abel, who grew up down the street in Clayton from Mavrakos Candy's last owner, Tom Wotka. Abel

Courtesy of Chocolate Chocolate Chocolate Company.

studied the recipes and reinvented a few for his company's product line.

With such steady growth, Chocolate Chocolate Chocolate Company had outgrown its manufacturing facility at the original Chippewa store. The company had been using the candy kitchen at Lake Forest Confections, 7801 Clayton Road. Abel and his friend, Lake Forest owner Bud Kolbrener, manufactured both brands from the kitchen in back of the European-styled candy store and bakery. Abel's company purchased Lake Forest in 2009.

Left to right: Dan Abel Jr., Christina Abel, Rosalie Abel, Dan Abel Sr., Christopher Abel. Courtesy of Chocolate Chocolate Chocolate Company.

Two years later, the Gourmet Wholesale Division was created, and in 2012, the new factory opened. Once a warehouse for the ***St. Louis Post-Dispatch*** newspaper, the 1950s-era building was totally rehabbed, said Dan Abel Jr., with construction taking about eight months.

"We started from scratch," he says. "We loved the building's layout and we loved being on The Hill. It was a perfect fit."

And while the family decided to open the facility for free tours, Abel said they had no idea how well the idea would be received. But on the day the building opened to the public, 475 people came for the tour. Abel said as many as 50,000 people a year have toured the factory since its opening. It's popular with school and senior citizen groups (the building is ADA accessible), but they also get a good number of visitors from other states, including Arkansas and Wisconsin.

Four factory lines can run at the same time, making dark, milk, or white chocolates, as well as various molds. Inside the candy kitchen, the fondants for various truffles are made, as well as caramels and English toffee, which takes four days to make. Abel said the factory's state-of-the-art machines can make a batch of truffles in about an hour, from coating to striping (decorating).

"It's really brought us to a new level," he says.

Yet, all natural ingredients are used in the candy. There's no artificial dyes in the heart-shaped red velvet truffles being made for Mother's Day; the colorful drizzles are made with beet and apple juices. There's no powdered milk in the milk chocolate; natural whole milk is blended with the dark chocolate.

Blocks of chocolate, blended to company specifications, are supplied to the factory from U.S. and Belgium sources and stored in the warehouse next door. About 20 percent of what's produced stays in the St. Louis area; the rest is shipped nationally for wholesale customers that include Macy's, and HomeGoods stores. Dierbergs Markets, a large regional grocer, is another big customer, as is Mariano's Markets in the Chicago area. The retail store on location has the best sales – not surprising, given the number of tours given per year – and each Chocolate Chocolate Chocolate store has a small kitchen to make candy. Abel said

during Valentine's Day, it's tough to keep their chocolate-covered strawberries in the cases, and people often wait in line for a fresh batch.

In fact, the strawberries are among the most popular items, and they are offered freshly made year-round. But the artisan truffles and sea salt caramels also sell very well. He enthusiastically shows me a sample of the caramels topped with red Hawaiian salt, flaked salt from Cypress, and naturally colored pink Himalayan salt.

"It takes a whole world to make the product," Abel says with a smile. "Pretty cool."

When asked what he loves most about his job, Abel said, "I've been obsessed with chocolate since I was 5 years old. I was always in the kitchen. Chocolate excites literally every sense you have. I thank God I'm doing what I love to do every day. It's a labor of love for us."

Chocolate Chocolate Chocolate Company
www.chocolatechocolate.com

Factory and store
5025 Pattison Ave.
St. Louis, MO, 63110
(314) 338-3501

Tours are offered from 9 a.m. to 3 p.m. Monday–Friday every 30 minutes (except from noon to 12:30 p.m.), and on Saturday by reservation from 9 a.m. to 1 p.m.

Retail stores are in south St. Louis, Kirkwood, Chesterfield, Florissant, St. Peters, and St. Charles in Missouri. Illinois locations are Shiloh and Edwardsville. See the website for more information.

Lake Forest Confections is located at 7801 Clayton Road, (314) 721-9997, www.lakeforestchocolates.com.

Connect with Chocolate Chocolate Chocolate Company on Facebook and Twitter.

Tasty Tidbits

A statue of an Italian immigrant family is one of the many landmarks in The Hill neighborhood. Courtesy of Missouri Division of Tourism.

The Hill Neighborhood

With its Italian flair, The Hill is one of St. Louis' most popular neighborhoods to visit, as well as to live in. Baseball legends Yogi Berra and Joe Garagiola grew up here.

There's a variety of Italian restaurants to enjoy, whether you want a hot salami sandwich or a multi-course dinner. Sign up for a walking tour to learn about the neighborhood's history and see its anchor, St. Ambrose Catholic Church. You might find a bocce ball tournament going on at a local bar, or sign up for a wine tour.

Retail shops include Vitale's Bakery, DeGregorio Foods, and Herbia for handcrafted soaps. It's all about *la dolce vita* on The Hill.

While visiting The Hill, you're not far from another top St. Louis attraction, the Missouri Botanical Garden (www.mobot.org).

For more information, visit the neighborhood association's website, www.thehill2000.org.

Amighetti's on The Hill has wonderful breads and baked goods. The café serves Italian sandwiches and salads. Courtesy of Missouri Division of Tourism.

Crown Candy Kitchen

St. Louis

It's raining and a tornado watch is in effect until the evening, but this typical St. Louis spring weather did not deter the faithful from lining up under the familiar green and white striped awning in Old North St. Louis. There is bacon to be savored and rich, thick malts to be slowly sipped. At historical Crown Candy Kitchen, it's hard to say if it's the hearty lunches, sinful ice cream concoctions, or the handmade chocolate candies that bring people here. During my rainy Saturday afternoon visit, it seems all of the treats play a part. Diners downed sandwiches, shakes and sundaes, but stopped by the candy counter on the way out the door.

Crown Candy is wrapped in a time warp. Everything about it looks to be from another generation, from its red brick building to the collection of antique Coca-Cola memorabilia and antique soda fountain inside, the memories are as thick as the shakes here. Even the street corner is a throwback to the time when St. Louis had two newspapers as an old *St. Louis Globe-Democrat* paper box stands rusting next to a stop sign.

But it's all part of the experience at this sweet St. Louis attraction. Go once and you'll be hooked. Some patrons have been coming here since they were teenagers.

We waited about 30 minutes for a booth. The place only seats about 30 to 40 people at a time. The two-person booth is a snug fit and the

bigger booths aren't that much larger, but customers are happy to cozy up to one another, sometimes getting the waitress to pull another chair for a fifth person to seat at the end of the table. She's happy to accommodate the requests, but doesn't engage in a lot of chit-chat because this place does very brisk business. Once seated, service was speedy and our drink order – a Dr. Pepper, a chocolate-banana malt, and a strawberry-banana shake – came lickety-split.

Speaking of licks, the malts and shakes come to the table in tall, cold metal cups. Anyone who can drink five of these 24-ounce beauties in 30 minutes gets the malts for free and their name inscribed on a plaque in the store. Only 30 have succeeded, though many have tried, including Adam Richman in 2009 (*Man v. Food,* Food Network), who had to stop after four.

Courtesy of Deborah Reinhardt.

After we snapped pictures of us slurping these ice cream drinks, the food soon came out. Crown Candy is known for its Heart-Stopping BLT, a sandwich aptly named, as it is piled so high with bacon, I had to wrestle it into my mouth. The sandwich won.

Crown Candy can fry about 200 pounds of bacon a day to satisfy hungry customers, many of whom have heard about the sandwich after it was named the best in America by Richman in 2012.

Enticing new generations of customers is a hallmark of Crown Candy's success. The business is more than 100 years old, so they have to be doing something right.

In 1913, Harry Karandzieff and his best friend Pete Jugaloff emigrated from Greece to St. Louis and opened their candy store/soda fountain at 14th Street and St. Louis Avenue. The Karandzieff family lived above the store. Harry's son, George, ran the business in the 1950s; he was the one who thought to serve hearty sandwiches along with the ice cream, shakes, and malts. George passed away in 2005. His son, Mike, lost a fight with cancer and died in 2012.

George's surviving sons, Tommy and Andy, along with their families, keep Crown Candy going. His wife and the family's matriarch, Bessie Karandzieff, is in the candy kitchen, especially during the busy season leading up to Easter when St. Louisans will drive from the suburbs – some 45 minutes or more away – for the signature molded chocolate bunnies, heavenly hash nests, marshmallow eggs, and more. Christmas candies are shipped around the country to people who seek a little taste of home.

Let's talk about the chocolate candy. The cases are crammed with goodies like chocolate-covered raisin clusters, chocolate-caramel-pecan clusters, chocolate snappers, milk and dark nonpareils, chocolate-covered caramels, chocolate cherry cordials, molasses puffs, and more. You won't find the artisanal truffles in exotic flavors, or sea-salted caramels. This is all about comfort, so take a bite, close your eyes, and go back to when you were 10 years old and a piece of chocolate from a candy store was a real treat.

Courtesy of Deborah Reinhardt.

Andy Karandzieff says batches of clusters, heavenly hash, and chocolate barks are made about four times a week. The Arch bars also are poured on site. Milk chocolate candies outsell the dark, Karandzieff said, but he makes the semi-sweet dark available to those who want it.

I sampled the heavenly hash and chocolate-caramel-pecan cluster. The marshmallow in the heavenly hash might as well have been made by an angel, it was so light and melt-in-your-mouth delicate. The caramel in the pecan cluster has just the right chewy consistency and is kissed with vanilla.

Karandzieff says his family has been asked many times over the years about expanding or moving Crown Candy, but the answer is always the same: no thanks.

"We've been on this corner forever and we're going to stay here," he says. "Out of town people want a mini-adventure. And there are a lot of local multi-generational families that come here. They brought their kids and now bring their grandkids."

With the chocolate, cream, sugar, and butter, the Karandzieff family mixes in a heaping spoonful of nostalgia into their confections, and that might be the most comforting ingredient of them all.

Crown Candy Kitchen
www.crowncandykitchen.net

1401 St. Louis Ave.
St. Louis, MO 63106
(314) 621-9650

Hours are from 10:30 a.m. to 8 p.m. Monday–Thursday; 10:30 a.m. to 9 p.m. Friday and Saturday; closed on Sunday.

For more information about Crown Candy, check out a book by Dr. John L. Olandi, *Sweetness Preserved: The Story of the Crown Candy Kitchen,* which is available on the Crown Candy website.

Connect with Crown Candy Kitchen on Facebook and Twitter.

Kakao Chocolate

St. Louis

With imposing office towers and official-looking government buildings, Clayton, Mo., looks like a typical modern business center. Men and women pour out of these buildings throughout the day as they rush to the next appointment or the next big business deal. But a veritable oasis from the daily grind stands in the middle of the wheelings and dealings. It's Kakao Chocolate on Forsyth.

St. Louis chocolatier Brian Pelletier is the man behind Kakao, and the store in Clayton is his third location in less than seven years.

A former marketing professional, Pelletier wanted a new career after 20 years. In 2008, a friend mentioned she had some chocolate-making equipment for sale, so Pelletier bought it and learned how to make chocolates from his friend.

"My passion found me," he says. "I like chocolate as much as anybody else, and I felt that people who knew about chocolate were open to trying something new."

He started selling his handmade chocolates at farmer's markets using locally sourced ingredients – such as cream, honey, and eggs – whenever possible. No artificial ingredients or colors are used. Things were going well enough to buy a location for his first store, and he chose a historical building in south St. Louis on Jefferson Avenue off Cherokee Street, well-known for its collection of interesting, funky boutiques and antique stores.

The Jefferson Avenue Kakao was a grocery store in another life, and the space would work well for the demonstration candy kitchen. It's important that customers can see the chocolates are made by hand, Pelletier says, and that they can talk to and ask questions of the workers making the candy.

"You can watch them, talk with them, and take pictures," he says.

The Jefferson store opened in May 2009. In 2011, a second location in Maplewood opened. In 2014, Kakao's third location in Clayton opened. He also has a specialty food store, Larder & Cupboard, in Maplewood about a block from Kakao.

When asked if all of this was in his original vision, Pelletier chuckles.

"Whenever I want a good laugh, I read my original business plan," he says. "Look, I have to earn a living, but I didn't understand how it would grow. A lot has changed and evolved along the way."

What hasn't changed is Pelletier's hands-on approach to making chocolate and running his shops. He works in the shops, goes to off-site events involving Kakao, and is involved in the popular chocolate tastings.

Tastings for eight to 30 people are offered at the Maplewood and Clayton locations every day but Sunday. The cost is $12 per person for a tasting Monday-Thursday or $15 on Friday and Saturday.

"For me, it's about the experience of

Courtesy of Deborah Reinhardt.

eating the chocolate," Pelletier says. "And meeting people is part of that experience."

And there's something new to taste every week as Pelletier and his team work on devising different combinations of tastes for truffles and other confections. Small batches of about 220 hand-dipped pieces are available until they are gone. Then, the process starts over.

On a recent visit to the Clayton shop, I had a sample of several truffles, caramels, and chocolate bark. I started with the most popular item, sea salt caramels. Smooth and well-balanced dark chocolate wraps around buttery soft caramel with perfect chewy consistency. No wonder this is popular with so many of his customers. The white chocolate caramels with black Hawaiian sea salt were a very pleasant surprise.

"I've tried a lot of caramels but ours are different. It tastes great," Pelletier says.

Then I moved around the plate to the Persian plum truffle, a new flavor only made that week that features locally made rose tea. The delicate fruit flavor was balanced well with a floral essence from the tea.

Next was the Turkish coffee truffle, which won a national Good Food Award in the confections category in 2015. This flavor of truffle is one of the standards always available in the shops.

Another standard truffle is the Chai tea. Pelletier said it was the first new recipe to be introduced in the shops. "I came up with it myself," he says. In one bite, I tasted a perfect blend of cardamon, cinnamon, and milk chocolate.

Dark chocolate bark had a surprising addition of white pepper. Beautifully satisfying, the pepper seemed to freshen the chocolate. I took a small bag home to enjoy while reading in the evenings.

And that's perhaps the really cool thing about Kakao; all of the candy is affordable, which makes it accessible to just about anybody interested in

Brian Pelletier, owner. Courtesy of Deborah Reinhardt.

enjoying fine handmade chocolates. During my visit, a mom came by and filled a basket with delicious treats to give to teachers for an end-of-school-year gift. Not 20 minutes later, an office worker popped in and left with a small bag to stash in the back of her desk drawer to keep the later afternoon doldrums at bay.

Pelletier says a blend of chocolate from Belgium, Switzerland, and San Francisco is used for his candy. Like Goldilocks who sought the perfect porridge, Pelletier was after the right combination of texture and value.

"It took a lot of different tries, but now we have a signature flavor that provides a smooth base at a good value," he says.

Yet, Pelletier says when he conducts a chocolate tasting, he always asks if anyone present is new to Kakao, and usually at least one hand goes up.

"That surprises me. But by the time we're done, they understand what we're doing. We have a lot of people we need to introduce to Kakao," he says.

He understands there are a lot of fine chocolatiers in St. Louis – some reaching for the stars and large, national markets, while others are satisfied to make fine confections for loyal but smaller customer bases. Pelletier says he wishes all of them well.

"But my goal is to make Kakao the reason people come to St. Louis," he says. "I have the best job in the world."

Kakao Chocolate
www.kakaochocolate.com

2301 S. Jefferson Ave.
St. Louis, MO 63104
(314) 771-2310
Hours are from 10 a.m. to 6 p.m. Tuesday–Saturday; closed Sunday and Monday

7272 Manchester Road
Maplewood, MO 63143
(314) 645-4446
Hours are from 10 a.m. to 7 p.m. Monday–Saturday; noon to 5 p.m. Sunday

7720 Forsyth Blvd.
Clayton, MO 63105
(314) 726-7974
Hours are from 10 a.m. to 7 p.m. Monday–Friday; noon to 5 p.m. Saturday and Sunday

Connect with Kakao on Facebook, Twitter and Instagram.

Oh Sheila Chocolates

St. Louis

The petite, attractive woman standing next to a table laden with enticing chocolate selections looks as if she stepped out of a 1940s MGM musical. Wearing a red-and-white polka dot dress and a silk flower tucked in her neat chignon, St. Louis chocolatier Sheila Kleinschmidt is ready for the Valentine's Day onslaught. For chocolate makers, holidays and special events, such as weddings and milestone birthdays, are – pardon the pun – their bread and butter. As an independent chocolatier who makes small batches of handcrafted chocolate truffles and other treats, Kleinschmidt – the force behind Oh Sheila Chocolates – has set up shop for the day at a florist's shop in University City, a suburb just west of downtown St. Louis. She has no store; instead, Kleinschmidt makes chocolates to order, holds events, makes appearances around holidays, and sells her candy in a handful of retail shops near her home.

While pinup is her hobby and style, chocolate is Kleinschmidt's passion, and her customers can see and taste that in every truffle she makes. The ganache centers have flavors such as strawberry cream, maple/whiskey/bacon, lavender, passion fruit, and rum chipotle. Special flavor requests are accommodated whenever possible.

Courtesy of Oh Sheila Chocolates.

Courtesy of Oh Sheila Chocolates.

"I can do pretty much whatever people want for an event," she says.

She uses 60 percent dark chocolate purchased from a local supplier. In fact, Kleinschmidt says she uses local ingredients in Oh Sheila Chocolates, purchasing local cream, spices, wine and other spirits – even lavender – from St. Louis area businesses. She uses fair trade cocoa when possible, but admits that for a small business, the cost can be prohibitive. Her packaging is made of recycled materials, which she says is important to her.

Kleinschmidt grew up in southern Missouri near a Mennonite community. Her parents and grandparents were farmers, so the slow food concept is more than familiar to her. She said she often was in the kitchen as a child. "I grew up when candy was a special treat for kids and chocolate was extra special," she says.

Kleinschmidt is a self-taught chocolatier, but also worked full-time for four years in the catering business. She specialized in pastries.

"But I wanted to do something more part-time with three kids in school, so I tried something on my own," she says. With a husband in the wine business,

Kleinschmidt started out doing wine and chocolate tasting parties. "We started small and it snowballed from there."

Four-and-a-half years later, she seems to be as busy as she wants to be.

Kleinschmidt rents professional kitchen space not far from her home. She now uses a machine to temper (melt) her chocolate correctly – when she started, the process was done by hand, which was a bit more hit-and-miss. "If you don't temper chocolate correctly, it may not harden properly," she says.

The ganache centers for her truffles are made by hand and are allowed to set a full day. She scoops a center, hand rolls it, and dips it into the dark, milk, or white chocolate. The truffles, Kleinschmidt says, are her trademark creations.

"They (her customers) love the truffles. There's no aftertaste and they taste really fresh.

"I have a lot of repeat customers who reorder for birthdays or whatever. I try unique flavors using liqueurs and spices all the time," she says.

The six-piece truffle box that I took home was like a little treasure chest I guarded as if it were gold. The rum chipotle truffle has the hint of a rum taste and just enough heat from the smoked jalapeno to surprise my palate. Passion fruit's creamy ganache is kissed with a sweet taste of the exotic. Each truffle is covered in rich, dark chocolate and provides a satisfying snap when I bite into the candy.

Kleinschmidt also makes vanilla caramels sprinkled with sea salt and chocolate-coated bacon. She says she's the only chocolatier in town that makes the chocolate bacon. For Valentine's Day, you can order a few chocolate bacon roses for your guy.

As an independent chocolatier, Kleinschmidt says her greatest challenge is getting the word out about her business.

"I am small and haven't done a lot of marketing. It's been largely word of mouth so far, but Webster Groves is an awesome community. It's a great place to have a business. I just started doing those few retail locations (in Webster Groves) because I know if product is too difficult to get, customers will go somewhere else," she says.

For now, Kleinschmidt is focused on devising her unique flavors in small, handmade batches for customers who can taste the care in each savored bite.

"I enjoy being creative, and really love it when people love the product. That makes me happy," she says.

Courtesy of Oh Sheila Chocolates.

Oh Sheila Chocolates
www.ohsheila.com

Where to buy:

The Novel Neighbor
7905 Big Bend
Webster Groves, MO 63119

KIND Soap Company
20 Allen Ave., Suite 105
Webster Groves, MO 63119

Robust Wine Bar
227 W. Lockwood Ave.
Webster Groves, MO 63119

Connect with Oh Sheila Chocolate on Facebook and Twitter.

Rick Jordan Chocolatier

St. Louis

Sandwiched between a long-established neighborhood tavern and a Panera Bread bakery/café is the space where chocolatier Rick Jordan makes his magic happen. In this unassuming suburban strip mall off busy Clayton Road in Chesterfield, Mo., one of St. Louis' affluent western suburbs, Jordan has what he calls a "boutique" and "lab space." It would be easy to drive by his business; only a simple sign that reads "chocolatier" crowns the entrance.

But chocolate devoteés in St. Louis know where to find Jordan – who was named one of North America's top 10 chocolatiers in 2013 by *Dessert Professional* magazine – for it is in this quiet suburban chocolate shop where they can find some of the most artful and delicious chocolate made in the area.

Jordan's bonbons are the color of jewels. In fact, a few years ago for Valentine's Day, he sold a box of white passion-fruit infused "demispheres" set on a red-tinted chocolate bar – the "pearl necklace."

On my visit, the chocolate collections are displayed on what could be a jewelry counter inside the sleek shop. A large window separates the small retail area from the work space. Sometimes, customers can find Jordan behind the glass creating his next batch of unusual chocolates.

As you'd expect from an artisan chocolate maker, Jordan uses natural ingredients – many locally sourced – for his creations. Part of his chocolate-making

Courtesy of Deborah Reinhardt.

process is roasting and grinding cacao beans himself to make the house chocolate blend, which during my visit was Cuyagua from Venezuela. Many of the beans come from the cacao plants he grows indoors in St. Louis. The honey in the wonderful honey caramels comes from his personal hives.

Honey-flavored caramel also can be found in the "honey demispheres," part of the Missouri collection, that features Missouri elderberry dark chocolate ganache and black walnuts.

In addition, there are chocolate bars and "snackables" that include almonds dusted in cocoa powder, chocolate crunch, caramels, and chocolate lollipops. There's something for any budget so just about anyone can indulge.

Like many other chocolatiers from the state, Jordan discovered his passion as an adult after realizing corporate life wasn't for him. He had several restaurant jobs – even opened a pizza place – before training at the culinary school in St. Louis, L'Ecole Culinaire. One of his instructors suggested Jordan extend his training at the French Pastry School in Chicago, which led to an opportunity to study in

France. He worked with chocolate artist Patrick Roger in Paris, whom Jordan refers to as "a chocolate god." That experience clarified for Jordan what he was meant to do – create fine chocolates – back in St. Louis.

Now, about four years into owning his chocolate business, Jordan continues to push the creativity envelope, without a lot of fanfare, from his chocolate laboratory. Then again, when chocolates are this delicious to look at and eat, one doesn't have to shout.

Rick Jordan Chocolatier
www.rjchocolatier.com

14882 Clayton Road
Chesterfield, MO 63017
(636) 230-9300

Hours are from 11 a.m. to 7 p.m. Monday–Friday (closed Mondays during summer) and noon to 7 p.m. on Saturday. Closed Sunday.

Connect with Rick Jordan Chocolatier on Facebook.

Riverside Sweets

St. Charles

The Missouri River, the "Big Muddy," flows past Frontier Park in St. Charles, Mo., connecting the city's storied past to its present. Fittingly, one of the park's features is a statue of explorers Meriwether Lewis and William Clark; the Corps of Discovery met up with Lewis in St. Charles in May 1804 to begin their historic trek to the Pacific coast.

Perhaps it's equally fitting that a lovely view of the river is offered to patrons of Riverside Sweets' ice cream parlor located in the lower level of its historical building. Riverside's owners, Jim and Kathy Brown – modern day adventurers – brought their family back east from Nevada to begin a new chapter in their family's life.

On a picture-perfect May afternoon, I met Jim Brown at his candy store. Wearing a Chicago Bears T-shirt, shorts, and running shoes, Brown explains he just returned from his daily run. "I do that so I can eat all of these goodies," he says with a grin.

Those goodies are tastefully displayed in cases and on numerous shelves throughout the warm and welcoming shop. His wife, Kathy, adds charming gift items – some locally made – and tucks them between bags of peanut brittle and other sweets. During the holidays and St. Charles' popular Christmas Traditions event, Brown says they do a brisk gift-buying business at the shop. The building dates to the 1860s, like many of its neighbors lining charming South Main Street.

I follow him down aged stairs to the ice cream parlor's space. While sampling some of Riverside's chocolate, we sit at a vintage metal table and chairs – so familiar to ice cream parlors of yesteryear – and I hear how the Browns wound up in this neck of the Midwest.

Courtesy of Deborah Reinhardt.

Originally from the Chicago, Ill., area, Brown worked for years in technical sales.

"I used to wear a coat and tie to work and went from one useless meeting to the next," he says. He eventually grew tired of the grind, and wanted to find a way to spend more time with his young family (the Browns have three children). They decided to go into business for themselves but wanted to purchase an existing business.

"We looked for a long time. Our criteria was simple; we wanted something the whole family could get involved in and we wanted an existing business," Brown says.

They also liked the Lake Tahoe area, which they were familiar with from vacationing there a few times. Then, a call came from their business broker. The owner of a candy store in Virginia City, Nev., was retiring and wanted to sell. The Browns bought the business, moved the family out West and opened Grandma's Fudge in 1994.

"All of a sudden, I'm wearing jeans and polo shirts to work," Brown says, adding that nobody in his family had experience making candy. "But you kill a couple of batches of fudge and that's how you learn." With determination and training from the shop's previous owner, the Browns learned well, and offered 30 varieties of homemade candy, including the fudge, at their shop.

They worked in Virginia City for about five years but eventually realized they missed Midwestern values and longed for home. One weekend while they were visiting friends in St. Charles, Kathy and a girlfriend were strolling Main Street shops and noticed a sign in a candy store window: "For Sale." Thirty days later, the Browns had bought the building and moved back to the Midwest within six months. Riverside Sweets opened in 1999.

Life's serendipitous moments indeed can be sweet.

"It was absolutely meant to be," Brown says.

The Browns' daughters – Kelly, Brittany, and Caitlyn – helped with the store. Caitlyn, who was 7 years old at the time, was given the task of standing on a crate behind the counter and greeting customers. Having a family business taught their children a strong work ethic, Brown says. Kelly, now married, still works with the family in the store. Caitlyn and her family live in Kansas City, Mo., where she works as a genetics counselor. Brittany is pursuing a graduate degree in Raleigh, N.C.

Making and selling candy is the primary focus at Riverside, where 85 percent of product is made on site, including all the fudge, brittles, and dipped chocolates. Cases display generously sized clusters (turtle, raisin or cashew), salted caramels, molasses puffs, various flavored brittles, and more. Caramel apples are offered year-round, and the chocolate strawberries are available "as long as they look good in the stores," Brown says. They use locally supplied cream and produce in their confections whenever possible. Chocolate is supplied from California and Chicago. Brown says they sell much more milk than dark chocolate.

More than a dozen different flavors of fudge are sold, but Brown's daughter, Kelly Stover, says the turtle fudge is a best-seller. The batch I tasted was smooth and melted in your mouth. Fudge is a sweet candy, and can sometimes make your

From left: Kelly Stover and Angela Wiechens. Courtesy of Deborah Reinhardt.

mouth pucker, but this was balanced just right. And the caramel running through each slice was a nice addition.

A nostalgic offering, divinity with walnuts, is another favorite. "Everyone says my grandmother used to make that," Brown says. "It's a lot of work to make, too. It's real tricky with the humidity here."

The ice cream parlor is open seasonally, April through October. Brown says they wanted to keep the old-fashioned feel to the parlor, which serves shakes, sodas, cones, and sundaes. In all, there are 24 flavors of ice cream (also available in the candy shop). It seems to click with his customers.

Brown remembers two patrons in particular, an elderly couple who lived in South St. Louis County (about 40 minutes from St. Charles). The couple drove to Riverside Sweets for ice cream six days a week and became like one of the family. Not long ago, their son, wanting his aging parents nearer to family, moved them back to Utah. Brown says they are missed.

And the gift items, which include a few cookbooks and decorations for home – are the final component to the shop.

Brown says the shop does well about 10 months out of the year, with post-Christmas winter months being slow. He doesn't have plans to expand into wholesale markets.

"We truly are a mom-and-pop business, but people like our style a lot," he says. "A lot of people who come in know us and we have a lot of regular customers. We're happy with that, and we'll keep it that way."

Riverside Sweets
www.riversidesweets.net

416 S. Main St.
St. Charles, MO 63301
(636) 724-4131

Hours: 10 a.m. to 5:30 p.m. Monday–Saturday; 11 a.m. to 5:30 p.m. Sunday. Parlor open from 12:30 to 5:30 p.m. Saturday and Sunday, spring through early fall. Summer has extended hours, so it's advisable to call before your visit.

Connect with Riverside Sweets on Facebook, Twitter, Pinterest, and Google+.

Tasty Tidbits

St. Charles

If historical, charming towns are your thing, you'll love visiting St. Charles. Founded by French Canadian fur trader Louis Blanchette, history here is tangible. See Missouri's First State Capitol, Lewis & Clark Boathouse and Nature Center, and other historical homes and museums. Daniel Boone Home and Heritage Center is not far in Defiance, Mo.

Most visitors will gravitate toward the river and Main Street. The southern half is filled with boutiques, restaurants, shops, and a winery. North Main, once offering mainly antique stores, now has a greater variety of shops, restaurants, bars, and a coffee house.

Hotels and charming B&Bs make an overnight stay easy and delightful, and special events throughout the majority of the year give greater reasons to visit this wonderful destination. For more information, visit www.historicstcharles.com.

First Capitol Building, St. Charles, Mo. Courstey of Missouri Division of Tourism.

Patric Chocolate

Columbia

Madame Jeanne Calment of Arles, France, ate almost two pounds of chocolate a day. She lived to be 122 years old. Supercentenarian Sarah Knauss, who lived in Pennsylvania, enjoyed snacking on milk chocolate turtles while watching television or needlepointing. She lived to be 119 years old.

Note to self: eat more chocolate.

And when the chocolate is as fine as Patric Chocolate, that won't be a problem.

Alan "Patric" McClure is the man behind Patric Chocolate, a craft chocolate company based in Columbia, Mo. McClure is one of only three "bean-to-bar" chocolate makers in Missouri.

Whether or not eating chocolate leads to longevity, we do know it has proven health benefits. Dark chocolate in moderation can improve heart and possibly brain health, thanks to flavanols, those wonderful little compounds that give cocoa its characteristic taste. A report out of Tufts University near Boston, Mass., stated flavanols in dark chocolate and cocoa "positively affect the circulatory system and help maintain the flexibility of the arteries."

Additionally, researchers from Boston's Brigham and Women's Hospital found a small group of subjects, averaging 73 years of age, improved cognitive skills with a daily intake of hot cocoa made from cocoa powder.

"Keep in mind that along with flavanol-packed cocoa in the candy or hot drink, typically there is also a good bit of fat, sugar, and other less healthy components,"

Courtesy of Deborah Reinhardt.

says University of Missouri Extension nutrition and health specialist Janet Hackert, who recommends eating no more than an ounce daily.

McClure, who recognizes chocolate as a "healthy food," founded Patric Chocolate in 2006 following about a year in France where he became familiar with the French chocolate-making traditions. After cocoa-sourcing trips to Mexico, Belize, and Venezuela and months of careful development in his new custom chocolate-making facility back home, he released his first bar, Madagascar, made with "single-estate" cacao and pure cane sugar in 2007. Single-estate or single-origin cacao refers to cacao beans grown in a particular area or the chocolate made from these beans, according to *The Nibble*, an online magazine devoted to specialty foods.

Although McClure, a Kansas City native, says he's done bonbons in the past for limited releases, "we do only bean-to-bar chocolate at this point." A bar is released each month, and when they're gone, that's it until the next release. McClure won't say how many bars he makes in a year, but customers can find his chocolate online or at a handful of Columbia retailers, including HyVee stores, Hoss's Market, and World Harvest Foods. The bars are also sold at Les Bourgeois Winery in Rocheport, Mo. Patric Chocolate does not have a retail space, but it does have 12 prestigious Good Food Awards.

One of those, the 67 percent Madagascar in 2013 won a Good Food silver medal in the plain chocolate category. It's a beautiful bar of dark chocolate with undertones of berries and citrus. It's sourced from a single orchard in Madagascar, and contains organic cacao, cane sugar, and cocoa butter.

Courtesy of Roger Meissen/MU Cooperative Media Group.

In 2013, Patric also released Holy Mole!, a permanent addition to its chocolate bar line. This 65 percent cacao bar uses cacao from Papua New Guinea and Ghana. If you can be disciplined enough to hold a piece of this chocolate on your tongue, you'll definitely experience the cinnamon and chiles. Smoked Spanish paprika and vanilla sea salt also are blended into the bar.

A limited-edition raspberry-balsamic pear bar was released in December 2014; it sold out in two days. Keeping up with demand keeps McClure and his several employees at the chocolate facility plenty busy, but the biggest challenge is "continuing to source quality cacao with complex and interesting flavor that can stand up on its own," he says.

Patric Chocolate
www.patricchocolate.com

6601 Stephens Station Road
Columbia, MO 65202
(573) 814-7520 (voicemail only)

There is no retail location here.

Connect with Patric Chocolate on Facebook, Twitter, and Instagram.

The Candy Factory

Columbia

Columbia is Missouri's quintessential college town. As home to the University of Missouri's flagship campus, the city has a special energy from the student population at MU and its unending cycle of young people moving in and out of town.

Mike Atkinson, owner of The Candy Factory, also moved in and out of Columbia, but a twist of fate brought him home.

Mike was 5 years old when his parents bought The Candy Factory in 1986. The Candy factory had been in existence since 1974.

Courtesy of The Candy Factory.

"Growing up, I worked at The Candy Factory helping to make simple items like chocolate-dipped pretzels or chocolate-covered graham crackers. I also had to do grunt work, like taking out the trash and recycling," he says.

When it was time to graduate high school, like most young people, Atkinson

Courtesy of The Candy Factory.

made plans to get out on his own and flex those freedom muscles. He left Columbia to study at Baylor University in Waco, Texas. Atkinson double-majored in marketing and entrepreneurship, making great plans for his future.

"At the time, I did not have any intention of moving back to Columbia and working in the family business," he says.

But like many graduates with a fresh degree and big plans, Atkinson had to catch the curveball life threw at him.

"After graduating and early into my professional life, my parents approached my wife, Amy, and me about taking over The Candy Factory," he says. In 2005, the couple moved to Columbia to start their careers at the chocolate shop. Neither had any culinary training.

Courtesy of The Candy Factory.

"Most of all the candy-making skills we have were learned on the job using techniques and recipes that had been perfected over the decades that preceded our careers at The Candy Factory," Atkinson says.

Indeed, for years, The Candy Factory has delivered marvelous candy, most of which is made on site at the downtown location using a variety of equipment, some dating to the 1950s. But Atkinson considers all of the confections to be handmade, as there is no fully automated machinery used in their process.

The jelly beans, gummi bears, and nostalgic confections are made by other companies and sold at the store, which also offers a selection of gift items.

But it's the chocolate confections that have been recognized among the best in the region. *Feast* magazine named The Candy Factory as the best confectioner in mid-Missouri. The noteworthy chocolate-covered strawberries were tagged as best chocolate dessert by *Inside Columbia* magazine. Indeed, the strawberries are one of the most popular confections sold at The Candy Factory, as are the sea salt caramels. *Midwest Living* called The Candy Factory a "Must Stop I-70 Attraction." And with a beautiful variety of fine chocolates, why wouldn't you pull off the highway?

Milk and dark chocolate truffles tempt with centers such as champagne, raspberry, tiramisu, or hazelnut. Katys – "turtles" – are made with Georgia pecans. English toffee, chocolate-covered cookies, pretzels – even potato chips – provide that satisfying crunch. New artisan chocolates present gorgeous, colorful molded shells with ganache centers that taste like pecan sticky buns or Bananas Foster. Then there's the chocolate pizza – a milk chocolate creation with marshmallow, cherries and a variety of nuts – that will quiet any chocoholic craving.

Good ingredients are the key to great candy, and it starts with the cocoa beans.

"The cocoa beans used in The Candy Factory's chocolate are sourced from South America. The relationship between the cocoa farmers and the company that makes our chocolate dates back over a century," Atkinson says.

Seasonal ingredients also play a big factor into The Candy Factory's quality product.

"Ingredient availability mainly affects what fruit we use," Atkinson says. "The Candy Factory makes double-dipped chocolate covered strawberries beginning the week of Valentine's Day and continues making them all year until mid-October when the quality of the strawberry crop diminishes.

"We make caramel apples August through October when we can find good, crisp Granny Smith apples. Chocolate-dipped raspberries are made all summer when the raspberry crop is plentiful. During the winter months when we cannot find good, fresh fruits, we focus on making gourmet popcorn."

Courtesy of The Candy Factory.

The quality and variety of chocolates are what The Candy Factory's broad customer base craves. In a way, being located in a city with a large student population has helped the business.

"One of the reasons we developed a shipping department back in the late 1980s, before shipping was automated and done by computers, was because The Candy Factory had such a great following and loyal customer base," Atkinson says. "When those customers moved away from Columbia, they told us that there was no other candy like ours in the new places they lived.

"So, to accommodate them, we began shipping our confections nationwide. Now, many local residents like to ship The Candy Factory's chocolates to their families as a source of pride to show off the quality of the confections they have in their hometown."

Courtesy of The Candy Factory.

It is the interaction with his customers that gives Atkinson the biggest thrill in his job, a job he hadn't planned on doing 10 years ago.

"I take a lot of joy when a customer brags on the candies we make, and take pride that The Candy Factory is a part of the community," Atkinson says. "It's almost as if we are a part of their families."

He says he also enjoys the professional interaction between confectioners.

"The candy-making community is a small one relative to other professional groups, so I really value the time I get speaking with and bouncing ideas off of other confectioners and chocolatiers.

"One of the biggest challenges in the business is to come up with new ideas. Chocolate and candy making has been around since the late 19th century, so coming up with new candies for our customers is a challenge, but one that I thoroughly enjoy."

The Candy Factory
www.thecandyfactory.biz

701 Cherry St.
Columbia, MO 65201
(573) 443-8222

Hours are from 9:30 a.m. to 6 p.m. Monday–Friday; 10 a.m. to 5 p.m. on Saturday; closed on Sunday.

Connect with The Candy Factory on Facebook, Twitter, Google+ and Pinterest.

Tasty Tidbits

Columbia, Mo.

The University of Missouri has a large presence in town, which fosters a healthy cultural environment. There's no shortage of art galleries, performances and festivals around town, as well as on campus.

Don't miss spending time to discover The District, a 50-square-block neighborhood nestled between three colleges that has fantastic shops, restaurants and nightlife. The energy here is palpable. There also are malls and shopping centers, farmers and flea markets, antique and boutique shops in Columbia for retail therapy.

Outdoor enthusiasts have parks, trails and the Katy Trail State Park to explore. Family fun, in addition to checking out the candy being made at The Candy Factory, includes bowling, rollerskating, movies and indoor arcades.

Grownups can check out Les Bourgeois Vineyards in nearby Rocheport, which offers tastings and fine dining with a great bluff view. Gaming is offered at Isle of Capri Casino in Boonville. Plenty of fine restaurants and music clubs are located throughout the city, so there will never be a chance to get bored on your visit.

For more information, visit the Columbia Convention and Visitors Bureau's website, www.visitcolumbiaMO.com.

University of Missouri Columbia campus. Courtesy of Missouri Division of Tourism.

Grandma's Candy Kitchen

Lake of the Ozarks

Many of us remember our grandmother as a woman who heaped gifts – praise, hugs and kisses, or food treats – on us. My mother once told me she had earned the right to spoil her grandchild just a little. I only knew my paternal grandma. My parents and grandparents lived together, and my grandma lavished me with attention and baked goodies.

For those who need a little grandmotherly TLC, Grandma's Candy Kitchen at Lake of the Ozarks in central Missouri can at least take care of heaping treats upon you. Step inside the cozy candy shop and be taken back to simpler days. Smell comforting aromas like vanilla. See baskets of favorite candies, such as salt water taffy, from your childhood. Of course, you can't miss the gleaming cases that are filled with fresh fudge. It's an astounding variety–20 flavors – and it's yours to enjoy. Go on, take a sample. Grandma would want you to.

Grandma's Candy Kitchen has been a part of Bagnell Dam Strip at the lake since the 1960s, according to Mike Page, who bought the business in 1992. Grandma's Candy is part of the Dogpatch attraction that dates to 1947.

Courtesy of Deborah Reinhardt.

Named for the fictional town in the Al Capp comic, "Li'l Abner," Walt Tietmeyer opened Dogpatch, a gas station and roadside stop at the time, anticipating leisure travel would boom following the post-World War II era. Tietmeyer believed the Lake of the Ozarks, created in 1931 by Union Electric – now Ameren Missouri – would be a part of the travel trend. He certainly called that one.

Page, who hails from Hannibal, Mo., but now lives at the lake, says Grandma's Candy had an "official grandma" in longtime employee Bernice Davis. While Page came with years of experience running various retail establishments, he was new to the candy business when he purchased Grandma's Candy Kitchen.

Courtesy of Deborah Reinhardt.

"We learned a lot from Bernice those first years," he says, adding that Davis passed away several years ago. Today's chief candy maker is Jenny White. Page employs up to 10 people during peak season. A seasonal business, Grandma's Candy closes in winter, which historically is a slower time for visiting the lake, with the exception of the holidays. Page says he's concerned about always serving the freshest candy possible, and with limited customers during the winter, the product would suffer.

As a seasonal business, summer is crunch time at Grandma's Candy. Twelve-hour days and all hands on deck are needed to keep up with demand.

"What we make today goes out the door by the afternoon," Page says. "It's quite an undertaking this time of year."

White and her crew during summer can make up to six kettles of fudge, with each kettle capable of turning out 36 pounds of the confection. That's almost 200 pounds of fudge in a day. He said chocolate fudge is the No. 1 seller, but the peanut butter-chocolate is a close second, with turtle fudge and dark chocolate sea salt caramel fudge (my favorite) gaining in popularity. During the busy season, a flavor of the month also is introduced. June brings wedding cake fudge. Watermelon-flavored fudge is the July offering.

"I love the seasonality of this business. You do work hard in the summer, but each day is a new start, each season brings something new. You look forward to it," he says.

But fudge is not the only chocolate treat you'll find at Grandma's Candy Kitchen. Page said the peanut clusters, turtles that are "chock-full of nuts" and sea salt caramels are popular items. More customers are discovering they like dark chocolate caramels and clusters, but Page says milk chocolate is most popular.

The taffy is not made on site, but comes from a supplier in Salt Lake City, Utah, Page says.

The longevity of Grandma's Candy stems from the fact that the shop focuses on fudge, a few well-loved chocolate candies, taffy, and a bit of the "penny candy," Page says.

"We try to do what we do well," he says. "We don't try to do everything."

That type of focus, plus the prime location and storied history are ingredients to continued success.

"We have customers who say they can't come to the lake without coming to Grandma's Candy Kitchen. For some, it's their first stop here," he says.

"The Strip" over the years has gone through change. Dogpatch may no longer feature piano-playing chickens and reptile gardens; businesses have come and gone. But the fact is at the lake, the Strip is one of the few places tourists can park their car and stroll from place to place, says Page, who also owns the Dogpatch souvenir store and the Leatherman shop on the Strip. He says the Strip is poised for new growth, with realty experts reporting renewed interest in investment opportunities. For Page, it's business as usual.

"We're satisfied with what we're doing. Hopefully, Grandma's Candy Kitchen will be around for another few generations; I think we're going to be here for quite some time," he says.

Grandma's Candy Kitchen
www.grandmas-candy.com

1470 Bagnell Dam Blvd.
Lake Ozark, MO 65049
(573) 365-2624

Hours are from 10 a.m. to 10 p.m. Memorial Day through Labor Day; 10 a.m. to 6 p.m. in spring and fall. Closed during winter months, reopening in early March.

Sweet on These Stops...

When you're exploring places in Central Missouri,
you'll be sweet on these chocolate destinations, too.

Cottleville, Mo.

VB Chocolate Bar, www.vbchocolatebar.com

It's almost closing time on Sunday night at VB Chocolate Bar in Cottleville, Mo. Just about everyone has cleared out for the evening except for a family of four finishing up their light supper in the dining room. At the opposite end of the building, two teenaged girls huddle over cups of coffee while discussing a Bible study. Two women have the outdoor patio all to themselves.

In the mid-17th century, chocolate houses – businesses where people gathered to enjoy chocolate drinks – were popular throughout Europe. Today, chocolate fans visit VBs, as it is know to the regulars, in St. Charles County to sip "boozy drinking chocolate" or chocolate martinis (the s'more martini is fantastic). VB Chocolate Bar reminds me a bit Europe's old chocolate houses in that it is a welcoming space for lovers of all things chocolate. It's not only a place where everybody knows your name, your barista knows how you take your latte and what truffle made by owner and chocolatier Conor Vanbuskirk will pair well with it. Chocolate-covered caramels and a variety of barks also are available.

Boozy ice cream floats (they make their ice cream on site), a large selection of beer, wines, and crafted cocktails, plus pastries, desserts (we tried the table side s'more) and a small but satisfying savory menu combine to make this an enjoyable destination for foodies of all sorts. You'll find VBs at 5326 state Highway N. The coffee bar is open daily; the chocolate bar is closed Mondays. For hours and more information, call (636) 352-1139. Connect with VB's on Facebook and Twitter.

Photos courtesy of Deborah Reinhardt.

Hermann, Mo.

Ricky's Chocolate Box

Photos courtesy of Deborah Reinhardt.

Hermann, Mo., is a fun day trip from St. Louis, but it's also a great wine country weekend escape. Located next to the tourism office, Ricky's Chocolate Box, 310 Market St., is a small yet completely worthy chocolate stop. I love the large truffles, pecan clusters, caramels, and other dipped treats. Ricky's does not have a website or any social media outlets, but call (573) 291-6107 for more information.

St. Louis, Mo.

Bailey's Chocolate Bar, www.baileyschocolatebar.com

The region's first chocolate bar opened in 2004. Owner David Bailey since has opened several restaurants in St. Louis that focus on affordable farm-to-table fare.

The chocolate bar in historical Lafayette Square is known for its variety of chocolate martinis and crazy good desserts. Try the signature chocolate martini with the chocolate caramel layer cake. Crafted cocktails and a great selection of beers and wine are offered at the bar, and a small menu of savory small plates also are available. But honestly, most folks come for the martinis and heavenly desserts.

Beer lovers may want to check out Bailey's Four Hands Brewery downtown on South Eighth Street. Some of the seasonal offerings at this craft brewery include the Chocolate Milk Stout, Bona Fide Imperial Stout, and Madagascar Milk Stout, all of which pair well with chocolate.

You'll find Bailey's Chocolate Bar at 1915 Park. The bar opens daily at 4 p.m. For hours and more information, call (314) 241-8100. Follow on Facebook.

St. Louis, Mo.

Merb's Candies, www.merbscandies.com

Since 1921, this family business has sweetened St. Louisans lives. I grew up near the South St. Louis store (4000 Grand Ave., 314-832-7117) It seems the Reinhardt's calendar wasn't driven by the usual forces; our seasons were defined by what was fresh at Merb's. Winter meant Heavenly Hash for Christmas and those ridiculously big chocolate-covered strawberries for Valentine's Day. In spring, I remember visiting with my mother before Easter to pick up the unbelievably good marshmallow and chocolate eggs. Mom bought several boxes at a time for us and for Easter gifts. My grandma liked to snack on the milk chocolate "snappers" (pecan and carmel clusters) while reading one of her Zane Gray novels on our screened-in back porch during early summer afternoons. Of course, autumn was time for the famous Bionic Apples.

Merb's offers creams, caramels, coconut and nut-filled chocolates. There are two additional locations in suburban St. Louis: the Sappington store is at 11644 Concord Village Ave. (314-843-7118) and the Ballwin location is at 14560 Manchester Road (636-230-9798). All three stores are closed Sundays.

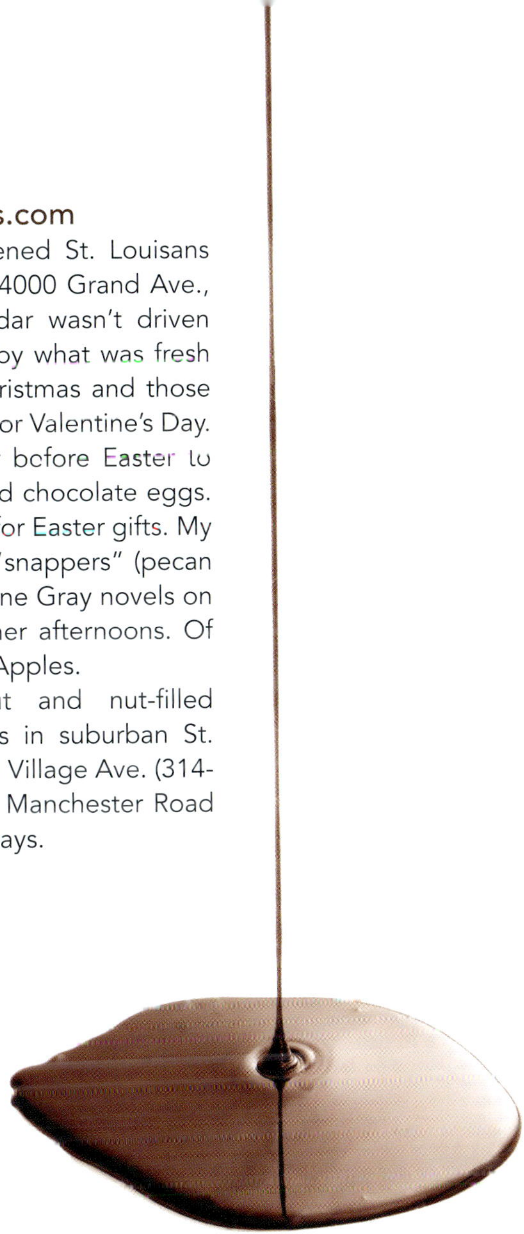

Southern Missouri

Corn and soybean fields, tent revivals and mega-churches, serene rivers and expansive lakes give southern Missouri its character. Mississippi River history and legends are alive in Cape Girardeau, while further south in Sikeston, a cotton festival is held every year.

In this region, travelers will also find wineries, the birthplace of Route 66, Civil War history, charming small towns, and the state's third-largest city.

Springfield

One of the state's best chocolatiers, Shawn Askinosie, hails from Springfield. His bean-to-bar chocolate business not only improves the lives of cacao farmers on four continents, but his philanthropic business model has garnered the attention of *The New York Times* and Oprah Winfrey.

Allow yourself to feel like that kid in the candy store again when you enter the Candy House Gourmet shop in Pinecrest Center. From cheerful wall colors to tantalizing candy counters, patrons can't help but leave with smiles on their faces (and bags of excellent handmade chocolate). Candy classes for children are a nice touch, too.

Elle Feldman's passion for fine living shines through in her purple-colored patisserie located in the charming Rountree neighborhood. Appreciating all things French, Feldman's shop is stocked with homemade pastries, macarons, truffles, marshmallows, and more.

While in Springfield, check out its historical downtown area, which offers an impressive selection of restaurants, shops, and art galleries. Antique lovers will want to see the massive Relics Antique Mall and Tearoom, while history buffs have Route 66 and Civil War sites to explore. During summer, visitors can see the Springfield Cardinals (the Double-A team of the St. Louis Cardinals MLB club) play at Hammons Field, while autumn and winter bring cultural offerings to the Juanita K. Hammons Hall for the Performing Arts.

Ste. Genevieve

History is alive every day in southeast Missouri's French colonial town, Ste. Genevieve. Ste. Genevieve's candy shop doesn't date to the 18th century, but it has operated under four owners since its founding in 1985.

As the name implies, Sweet Things Sweet Shop is all about candy. A mother-daughter duo, Joy and Nichole French, have been the owners since October 2013. Come in for nostalgic sweets and hand-dipped chocolate treats.

Charming Ste. Genevieve is packed with delightful restaurants, shops and B&Bs. Time your visit to catch one of the town's many festivals, including the popular Jour de Fête, the largest outdoor arts and craft fair in southeast Missouri, which is held annually in August. While in the area, make time to visit the fine wineries along the Route du Vin.

Slow down to savor the diverse activities and attractions that southern Missouri offers to travelers.

Askinosie Chocolate

Springfield

I was in line waiting to pay for gas one morning, when the man in front of me finished his transaction and turned around. Suddenly, I was face to face with Ozzie Smith, the St. Louis Cardinals Hall of Fame shortstop. In my best tongue-tied manner, I stood there wide-eyed, trying to force something – anything – out of my mouth, but not even a "Good morning, Mr. Smith" would come. Then, with a look on his face that said, "Yeah, I get that a lot; don't sweat it," Ozzie smiled at me and walked out the door.

I froze, trying to think of something new, clever, or inspiring to say to this St. Louis baseball legend, but I had nothing.

Brain freeze is setting in once again as I attempt to write about Askinosie Chocolate, a highly respected, Springfield-based artisan chocolate company. The bean-to-bar chocolate consistently wins national and international awards, and the company's socially responsible business model, A Stake in the Outcome™, has been featured in *The New York Times*. *O, The Oprah Magazine* named CEO and founder Shawn Askinosie "One of 15 Guys Who Are Saving the World."

If you're on Oprah's list of people who are making a difference and in the *Times,* you sure don't need me to help tell your story.

But what I find most inspiring about the Askinosie Chocolate story is an everyday guy, tired of his high-pressure career in law, taking a chance to pursue what makes him happy, hoping he

can make a go of it. Treating others with respect and kindness, he blesses those with whom he works, and the business thrives.

I mean, this is a Hallmark movie waiting to be made.

Askinosie's journey from the courtroom (he was a criminal defense lawyer) to a chocolate factory began in the late 1990s when he started cooking and baking as a stress-relieving hobby.

"I knew without a doubt that if I didn't quit, it (the job) was going to kill me," Askinosie says. "So I prayed a simple prayer nearly every day for five long years: Dear God, please give me something else to do."

So, for a year, he researched chocolate and how to make it from scratch. Later, in 2005, he flew to the Amazon rainforest to take a master class in cacao agronomy. He visited a chocolate factory in Ecuador to learn the craft. A year later, he and his family bought a building in a blighted area of Springfield, installed equipment, and perfected their chocolate-making

Courtesy of Askinosie Chocolate.

techniques at home and at the factory. They sold their first chocolate bar in 2007.

From the beginning, Askinosie wanted to make excellent chocolate in a fair and sustainable way while enhancing the community. Askinosie Chocolate claims to be the only chocolatier to practice direct trade on four continents. Lives have been changed in Springfield, as well as in Ecuador, Honduras, Tanzania, and the Philippines. Thus, his customers can feel good about enjoying his all-natural chocolate.

For example, take a look at the award-winning 72 percent dark chocolate Mababu bar.

Tanzania's Mbeya region has a strong cocoa bean cooperative, and Askinosie was the first chocolatier to trade directly with these cocoa farmers. The company sought a woman-led farmer group, and the photo of Mama Rahabu, who was the cooperative's leader, is pictured on the bar's package. (Mama Mpoki is the cooperative's new chairwoman.) In fact, each of Askinosie's bars present information and a photo of one of the farmers with whom Askinosie Chocolate partners.

Wait, it gets better.

The Mababu bar is a product of Chocolate University, a program for Springfield high school students that teaches participants how to become good global business people. By making artisan chocolate, Askinosie demonstrates to these young people that businesses can help solve the world's problems. He selects a few students to travel with him and daughter, Lawren, to Tanzania every other year.

Askinosie Chocolate has funded a deep-water well and begun a sustainable lunch program at a secondary school in this region of Tanzania. During an "origin trip" to the African country in July 2015, Shawn and Lawren presented cash to the cooperative's leaders, along with the profit-sharing statement that they translated into Swahili. After the agreement for the new year was signed, everyone enjoyed a beach party next to Lake Nyasa.

The bar that Askinosie Chocolate produces using these farmers' cocoa beans is a treasure. The velvety, rich chocolate is infused with a hint of fruit (like strawberry jam), which can be detected if you're disciplined enough to let the small chocolate square melt in your mouth. Hold it to up to your nose and take in the aroma. It's nearly a religious experience for any chocolate lover.

In an important partnership with a national retailer, Askinosie Chocolate was invited by Target to participate in their Made to Matter, Handpicked by Target™ collection highlighting businesses that "offer better choices." Three chocolate bars made from Tanzania cocoa beans were offered in select Target stores nationwide.

According to Askinosie, the partnership was about sharing the company's story and craft chocolate with a wider audience. Askinosie Chocolate was the first craft chocolate company picked by Target.

"Our collection with Target reflected the same integrity fans are used to with our chocolate: the beans were directly

Shawn Askinosie. Courtesy of Askinosie Chocolate.

Courtesy of Askinosie Chocolate.

sourced from our farmers in Tanzania, including our profit sharing program with those farmers, and we handcrafted everything in our factory with the same dedication to quality that our customers know and love," Askinosie said.

In addition to the variety of chocolate bars, Askinosie sells cocoa powder, baking chocolate, and roasted nibs, which can be enjoyed out of the can. Several chocolate gifts – such as the chocolate-tasting kit featuring four distinct bars, tasting instructions and a flavor wheel – are also sold online.

Askinosie's factory in Springfield offers tours every Tuesday at 3:30 p.m. The fee – which supports Chocolate University – is $5 for adults and $4 for children.

On select Saturdays in December, Shawn leads tours for the holidays, which is kind of a big thing, considering he's often flying to four continents on origin trips, accepting awards, or traveling around the country for speaking engagements.

The factory also offers a tasting bar and sells chocolate and gift items on-site.

In less than 10 years, the impact and reputation this small Missouri business has made around the world – as well as in Springfield – is nothing short of inspiring and remarkable. Social responsibility is not a buzzword for Shawn Askinosie.

"It's who we are," he said. "Askinosie Chocolate was born committed to fairness, sustainability, minimal environmental impact, and community enhancement. Those commitments will be in place as long as the company is.

"We're dedicated not just to making the best quality chocolate you can buy, but to making it in such a way that the more you learn about it, the better you feel about it."

Askinosie Chocolate
www.askinosie.com

514 E. Commercial
Springfield, MO, 65803
(417) 862-9900

Store hours are 10 a.m. to 5:30 p.m. Monday–Thursday; 10 a.m. to 5 p.m. Friday; 11 a.m. to 3 p.m. Saturday.

Connect with Askinosie on Facebook, Twitter, Youtube and Instagram or subscribe to their chocolate blog.

TASTY TIDBITS

Springfield, Mo.

Missouri's third-largest city has something for everyone to enjoy. This Southwest Missouri destination has Civil War history, plus plenty of Route 66 lore. The newly expanded History Museum on the Square gives a good snapshot of the region.

Sports fans can visit the Springfield Cardinals at Hammons Field or check out the Missouri Sports Hall of Fame. Family-friendly activities include exploring some of the beautiful parks, Dickerson Park Zoo, the Discovery Center of Springfield, and Fantastic Caverns. Bass Pro Shop Outdoor World – the mother store – is one of the top Springfield attractions.

Chocolate-loving travelers have plenty to enjoy in Springfield, too. For those who also love antique shopping, stop by Relics Antique Mall and Tearoom (2015 W. Battlefield) and browse more than 2,000 pieces of American, British, and French antique furniture and much more in the super-sized mall featuring hundreds of dealers. Try the homemade chicken salad and apricot-mango iced tea, but save room for the Chocolate Flourless Torte.

Fans of craft breweries will want to taste Chocolate Thunder at Mother's Brewing Company, which is made, in part, using nibs from Askinosie Chocolate.

No matter what interests drive your visit to Springfield, consider a stay at the new Hotel Vandivort (305 E. Walnut). Originally built as a Masonic Temple, the 108-year-old structure has been artistically transformed into a 50-room boutique hotel. With its downtown location, Hotel Vandivort is within walking distance to several attractions; it's next door to the Historic Landers Theatre.

Be sure to enjoy the hotel's restaurant, The Order, which features culinary creations by Chef Zach White using ingredients from local farms. Everything I sampled was superb, from the selection of appetizers to the Cast-Iron Crispy Skin Chicken, but be sure to save room for the Chocolate Pot de Creme, made with Askinosie dark chocolate – it may change your life.

You also can simply enjoy one of the many crafted cocktails in the lobby and watch the endless parade of people.

For more information, visit the Springfield Convention & Visitors Bureau's website, www.springfieldMO.org.

Elle's Patisserie

Springfield

You know, the French really *get* the food thing.

It's not about quantity, it's all about quality. Food isn't gulped down while dashing to chauffeur kids between sports and gymnastics lessons; it is celebrated and savored. And sweet things are not avoided, but rather embraced.

Thank goodness Elle Feldman also gets it. Her darling purple patisserie in Springfield's Rountree neighborhood (at the intersection of Pickwick and Cherry) is a shining beacon to the French philosophy of eat well, laugh often, and love abundantly.

Courtesy of Elle's Patisserie.

Feldman doesn't hail from Paris, but her days as a flight attendant allowed her to travel. While she'd wait in New York City for her next flight assignment, Feldman, then newly married, would buy cookbooks and teach herself to cook, as well as make truffles.

In 2005, Feldman and her husband, Jon, moved to

Springfield, where he was born and where his father currently lives. The couple met in 1993 while attending college in St. Louis, where her husband grew up. Their son, Oliver, was born in 2007.

Now a wife and mother, Feldman took on a new career as an esthetician. She opened Lavare Spa in town and began to include homemade truffles for her facial clients. Over the years, the demand for her truffles grew, along with her reputation as a fine esthetician, and on Valentine's Day 2011, she opened the patisserie, which is next door to her spa.

The signature lavender color of the small building's exterior was inspired by her time in France, where Feldman completed skin-care and aromatherapy training. In the little town of Sault near Mont Blanc, Feldman noticed that color purple on a garage door and shutters.

"Once we painted the building, I noticed the color was also my favorite color as a teen," she says. "I remember having a lipstick that color in the 1980s."

Her travels also inspire her treats. In 2015, Feldman and her husband were in Paris in January, Venice in March, and San Francisco in August. She calls it "treat research."

"I'm most inspired by life and food I've experienced," Feldman says.

That includes her childhood. Though a self-taught chef, Feldman says she has loved baking most of her life.

Courtesy of Deborah Reinhardt.

"I've been baking since I can remember with my grandmother," she says. "All the women in my life have inspired and taught me how to bake." Feldman learned how to make some candy by deconstructing all the treats she liked to eat. Other times, she simply asked for recipes.

Elle Feldman. Courtesy of Elle's Patisserie.

"I asked my Aunt Diane how to make potato candy and my friend's mom, Mrs. Kreutz, how to make her Rocky Road Bars, my favorite thing that we make," Feldman says.

In addition to the women within her circle of friends and family, Feldman's culinary inspirations include San Francisco's Joseph Schmidt and Pierre Hermé in Paris. Hermé, whom *Vogue* referred to as "the Picasso of Pastry," is most famous for his *macarons*. Although Joseph Schmidt Confections ceased operation in 2009, his egg-shaped truffles had Feldman's devotion at first bite.

"The first truffles I fell in love with were made by Joseph Schmidt," she says.

European influences are noticeable not only within Elle's pastry and candy cases, but outside the patisserie, too. In 2015, a "major exterior refresh" was completed. It includes a charming courtyard with a provincial fountain as its centerpiece and bistro tables and chairs that provide seating for customers to enjoy a pastry, French-pressed coffee, ice cream or a truffle.

And the truffles are large enough to enjoy in several satisfying bites. There are a few dozen flavors, but because the truffles are made by hand in small batches, not all flavors are available each day. There are no preservatives in the truffles, and each box is stamped with an expiration date, although I cannot imagine these little treasures not being enjoyed within a few days.

Newer flavors include Key lime, lemon, and spicy chili. Not straying from tradition, I tried the white-chocolate almond truffle. A smooth, white-chocolate ganache supported the almond flavor quite well, while the dark chocolate on the outside gave the truffle a rich finish. The champagne truffle was beautiful to look at – its white exterior dusted with gold flecks – but I couldn't pick up the champagne in the chocolate ganache center. Still, it was a delicious treat.

Feldman says the best-selling truffle is the salted caramel. I can see her point; that sweet and salty balance is wildly popular with so many chocolate lovers. It's quite good. She also sells a good amount of the dark-chocolate ganache with white chocolate and Askinosie cocoa nibs.

"We use Belgian couverture chocolate because it is the ultimate for truffle-making," Feldman says. "I make signature truffles and macarons using locally sourced boutique chocolate from Askinosie. We use locally sourced dairy and eggs when we have access to it."

Courtesy of Deborah Reinhardt.

As amazing as the truffles are, Feldman says her favorite treats are the Rocky Road Bars. "Those are my weakness. I also love my husband's macarons," she says. But a pinch of Askinosie's dark milk chocolate satisfies her sweet tooth, too.

With awards from Springfield's Drury College, Milwaukee's Alverno College and the Springfield Art Museum for her enterprise and chocolate-making skills, the word about Elle's Patisserie continues to spread throughout the Midwest. And for this busy entrepreneur/wife/mother, the biggest challenge of owning a patisserie is finding enough hours in the day.

"We do it all. It's long days on our feet, but it is a labor of love," she says. "And I love making truffles the most. Making truffle ganache is mesmerizing. Watching the cream and chocolate melt into shiny, smooth ganache is beautiful. I can make truffles for hours. It's calming to be in my kitchen alone, playing with chocolate."

Elle's Patisserie
www.ellespatisserie.com

1454 E. Cherry St.
Springfield, MO 65802
(417) 832-2171

Hours are 7 a.m. to 2 p.m. Tuesday–Thursday; 8 a.m. to 9 p.m. Friday and Saturday; closed Sunday and Monday.

Check out Elle's Patisserie sweets and French baguettes on Saturdays at the Farmers Market of the Ozarks in Springfield, 2144 E. Republic Road.

Connect with Elle's Patisserie on Facebook.

Tasty Tidbits

Rountree neighborhood

In Springfield's city center, near Missouri State University, Rountree is a pretty little neighborhood where a visitor could easily spend a full afternoon.

At Tea Bar & Bites Bakery and Café, 612 S. Pickwick, Colleen Smith has presented a well-rounded menu for a loyal customer base for 11 years. Pop in for a pastry in the morning, try a salad for lunch or one of about four entreés offered on their changing dinner menu. Catch live music on select Thursday nights or admire the local artwork featured on her café walls that month. There's also a wonderful courtyard attached to the small café; if the weather is good, by all means, dine al fresco by the courtyard fountain.

At the end of the courtyard you'll find Zen 3 Spa and Bodyworks, a sweet day spa offering a good selection of treatments for men and women, as well as yoga classes. Feel a bit like you're on vacation by taking one of the massage treatments outside on the spa's private deck, which overlooks Smith's well-cultivated gardens.

Foodies will also appreciate Homegrown Food, a local market (607 S. Pickwick) selling locally sourced meat, dairy, produce and more. Ott's Pasta, 1437 E. Cherry, is a carry-out pasta eatery that has a popular three-cheese house casserole. Entree, salad and bread are packaged for under $5.

For more information, visit www.RountreeNews.org.

Candy House Gourmet

SPRINGFIELD

From the outside, Candy House Gourmet in Springfield's Pinecrest Center looks like any of the pleasant storefronts in this suburban strip mall. But step inside and you'll instantly see what this store is selling. Sure, there's a great selection of chocolate, candies, and other treats, but what Candy House Gourmet is *really* selling is happiness.

From the abundantly cheerful aproned clerk who trots over with a smile asking, "How can I help you today?" to the colorful jars of gummy bears by the door, Candy House Gourmet is a giant smiley face. If you don't leave here with a grin on *your* face, it is time to seek therapy.

In a weird way, Candy House Gourmet reminds me of my aunt, a woman of style and taste who, each time we visited her house, had a spotless home and a delicious, artfully prepared dinner on her inviting table.

Courtesy of Deborah Reinhardt.

You were always welcome at Aunt Georgia and Uncle Lee's house, so we'd walk in and make ourselves comfortable.

There's a similar sense of familiarity at Candy House Gourmet, even during my first visit. The shop's thoughtful design leads me first to the wooden and glass cases topped with jars of chocolate almonds and malt balls, with beautifully formed truffles winking at me from below. Next, I make my way to the case with nut and raisin clusters and the like. In the middle of the store, waiting in cute, flat baskets, are bags of the popular English toffee, chocolate lollipops, beautifully boxed sets of chocolate that scream "perfect hostess gift," and gourmet popcorn in all colors of the rainbow.

In the fall, you'll find caramel apples, and for Valentine's Day as well as Mother's Day, hand-dipped chocolate-covered strawberries are the star attraction. But no matter the season, you'll always see a small tray on the front counter with free chocolate samples.

It all looks so effortlessly put together, but as my auntie could tell you, years of practice and a good deal of hard work happen in the background before anybody can enjoy hospitality.

I bet Candy House Gourmet owner Bonnie Nolen would agree.

She explains Candy House Gourmet began as Richardson's Candy House in 1970 in an old rock tavern south of Joplin, Mo. Don and Peggy Richardson were the proprietors, and they used recipes from Peggy's mom, Dolly, who

Bonnie Nolen. Courtesy of Deborah Reinhardt.

had a candy store in Florida.

In 1999, Nolen's parents, Terry and Pat Hicklin, purchased Candy House. A few years later, the family opened the chocolate factory in downtown Joplin, which offers tours. The Springfield store opened in 2002.

Courtesy of Deborah Reinhardt.

All the chocolates are made at the factory, and Nolen says they offer more than 75 varieties of truffles, barks, and other candies. The Candy House, Nolen says, is best known for their English toffee, caramel pecan treats, and sea salt caramels.

"There is definitely something for everyone," she says. "My favorite piece of candy we make is called Mine Run. It is named that because Joplin was a mining town. It is gold on the inside with a malt ball texture and a molasses flavor." She said other candy companies may call it molasses puffs.

The English toffee and sea salt caramels are delicious. I liked the consistency of the toffee – just enough buttery crunch without breaking off a tooth. I defy anyone to eat only one piece out of a bag.

I also buy a small bag of four truffles. One has a mocha ganache center enrobed in dark chocolate and then milk chocolate, a different, but welcome, approach. Another, a dark chocolate mint, is a little light on the mint for my taste, but the milk chocolate caramel truffle hit it out of the park.

"We have just started to offer our chocolate truffles made with all-natural ingredients and covered in chocolate that is made with certified fair-trade cocoa," Nolen says. "We're very excited about this new addition to our chocolate family."

In fact, coming up with new candies is the best part of Nolen's job.

"We're getting ready to introduce candied bacon to our Springfield store," Nolen says. "It's delicious and so different than anything we've offered before."

Candy House Gourmet
www.candyhouse.net

3857 S. Campbell
Springfield, MO 65807
(417) 883-3900

Store hours are 9:30 a.m. to 6 p.m. Monday–Saturday; 12:30 p.m. to 5:30 p.m. Sunday. Candy classes are frequently offered for children at this site.

Chocolate Factory
510 S. Kentucky
Joplin, MO 64801
(417) 623-7171

Hours are 9:30 a.m. to 5:30 p.m. Monday–Saturday; 9:30 a.m. to 6 p.m. Sunday. Call (877) 623-7171 for factory tour times and reservations.

Redings Mill Historic Store
454 Redings Mill Road
Joplin, MO 64804
(417) 624-1515

Store hours are 9:30 a.m. to 5:30 p.m. Monday–Saturday; 9:30 a.m. to 6 p.m. Sunday.

Connect with Candy House Gourmet on Facebook, Twitter and Pinterest.

Sweet Things Sweet Shop

Ste. Genevieve

History isn't just a book of static facts and dates in Ste. Genevieve, Mo. Here, history lives and breathes. Visitors to Missouri's oldest town can see 18th-century buildings and catch historical interpreters demonstrating ways of life from the French colonial era.

French Canadian settlers founded the village in 1735. It was one of several important French communities that were part of "Illinois Country," until 1762, when France ceded all of its land west of the Mississippi River to Spain after the French and Indian War. Despite Spanish control, Ste. Genevieve retained its French language and character.

Courtesy of Deborah Reinhardt.

After a monumental flood in 1785, the village was moved to higher ground, its present location in

Courtesy of Deborah Reinhardt.

southeast Missouri off state Route 32. In addition to seeing several historical homes in town, visitors enjoy browsing the collection of interesting shops.

One such shop is Sweet Things Sweet Shop. As the name implies, Sweet Things is all about candy. It doesn't date to French colonial times, but it has operated under four owners since its founding in 1985. A mother-daughter duo, Joy and Nichole French, have been the owners since October 2013.

The shop's darling white-washed brick building dates to 1860. Enter through the pink and white door and see a small but cheery store packed with candy and gifts, some of which are made by Joy and Nichole.

Daughter Nichole says her mom retired in 2009 after 30 years as an art teacher and relocated from Vibernum, Mo., to Ste. Genevieve. Nichole graduated from Missouri Baptist College in St. Louis, Mo., with a degree in education in 2011. According to Nichole, Joy has always been good at crafts – including basket-making and chair-caning – and dreamed of owning a little shop.

When the women learned the Sweet Things store was up for sale, they discussed going into business together. Nichole was working as a substitute teacher at the time. The store had an established customer base, plus Ste. Genevieve was one of Missouri's popular tourist stops, so it seemed like the timing was right to make a move.

"I do the daily management of the store," Nichole says. "Mom does baskets and crafts and some of the candy on the side."

Because of the small size of the shop, they make only the dipped Oreo cookies, pretzel rods, and smaller orders for chocolate-covered strawberries on-site. The back room is used as an office and storeroom, so they use their church's kitchen to fill Valentine's Day orders for strawberries.

"This year, we made 60 dozen chocolate strawberries. That was insane," Nichole says.

The rest of their candy – including chocolate mints, truffles, double-dipped peanut clusters, and caramels – are purchased from wholesale candy makers located in the Midwest, Texas, and as far away as California. Nichole says none of the previous owners made candy on-site because there simply isn't a properly equipped kitchen.

Nichole French. Courtesy of Deborah Reinhardt.

But that doesn't stop the loyal customers from coming back for their favorites, such as Knudsen's wrapped caramels from Minnesota. "We sell a ton of them," Nichole says.

The collection of nostalgic candies many baby boomers remember from childhood is also popular.

Nichole says "it's been an interesting two years" as she and her mom learn the seasonal rhythm of the candy-store business. They took ownership of the store just before Halloween and faced the Christmas shopping onslaught with barely enough time to come up for air before Valentine's Day, followed by Easter. Remembering those harried days, Nichole simply says, "Yeah."

Now that the first few years are in the books, this mom and daughter are looking forward to keeping the sweet tradition of a hometown candy shop going strong.

"We've had so many people tell us 'I'm so glad the shop is still here,'" Nichole says. "When people walk through the store, they remember all the candy from their past."

And that's proof that history isn't always found in books. Sometimes it is rediscovered in a bright pink candy wrapper.

Sweet Things Sweet Shop
www.stegencandy.net

242 Market St.
Ste. Genevieve, MO 63670
(573) 883-7990

Hours are 10 a.m. to 5 p.m. Monday–Saturday; 12:30 p.m. to 3:30 p.m. on Sunday.

Connect with Sweet Things Sweet Shop on Facebook, Twitter and Instagram.

TASTY TIDBITS

Ste. Genevieve

Charming Ste. Genevieve is packed with delightful restaurants, shops and B&Bs. There are events throughout the year, but chocolate lovers will want to visit around Valentine's Day to participate in the Chocolate Walk. Downtown businesses offer luscious chocolate treats during the walk, and shoppers purchase a $10 ticket to sample the sweet offerings at each participating business.

If you love sampling wine, there are 10 wineries throughout the Ste. Genevieve area to enjoy.

Meanwhile, history buffs will never be at a loss for something to do here. Explore nine wonderfully preserved historical buildings, including the 1792 Bolduc House Museum and the 1818 Felix Vallé House State Historic Site.

For more information, visit the Department of Tourism website, www.VisitSteGen.com.

Visitors at the Felix Vallé House State Historic Site in Ste. Genevieve enjoy French colonial programs. Courtesy of Missouri Division of Tourism.

Sweet on These Stops...

When you're exploring places in Southern Missouri, you'll be sweet on these chocolate destinations, too.

Phillipsburg, Mo.

Redmon's, www.redmonscandy.com

Location, location, location. The time-tested real estate adage rings true for this candy stop off Interstate 44 in southwest Missouri.

The small town of Phillipsburg lies between Rolla and Springfield. Redmon's opened in 1995. John and Sharon Redmon wanted to offer a clean, comfortable rest stop for the millions of tourists making their way to Springfield and Branson, plus points west.

Chocolate favorites – such as homemade fudge, turtles, peanut butter cups and haystacks – are made on-site. In addition, tourists will find more than 70 flavors of salt water taffy and an equal variety of nostalgic candy sold in bulk. All this, plus the entertaining billboards seen for about 30 miles on either side of Phillipsburg, make a strong case to stop off the road at Redmon's, which is open daily. While you can see the store immediately off the exit, the physical address is 330 W. Pine St. For more information, call (417) 589-2123.

Will Brake for Chocolate

Missouri road trips always include a wide variety of regional foods, from award-winning Kansas City barbecue to crazy concrete shakes on Route 66 in St. Louis.

If you're exploring Branson, one of Missouri's busiest tourist areas, chances are you will find a chocolate destination of one kind or another. These nationally franchised stores often hail from another state, but offer chocolate lovers copious choices to sweeten their vacations.

Branson Landing

On the Taneycomo lakefront in downtown Branson is the popular Branson Landing shopping and dining attraction. Anchored by Bass Pro Shops on one end and Belk department store on the other, Branson Landing is filled with national brands, galleries and retail specialty shops, including several candy stores.

Kilwins, www.kilwins.com

Hailing from northern Michigan, Kilwins' first store opened in 1947. Today, more than 80 franchise stores are scattered throughout the country; two are located in Missouri, including the store at Branson Landing. The other store is in St. Charles, 300 S. Main St.

Kilwins offers tasty chocolate with a touch of nostalgia. Not everything is made on-site. The chocolate truffles, toffee, creams, clusters and "tuttles" (turtle-style caramel, chocolate and nut candies) and single-origin chocolate bars are made in the Michigan factory and shipped to franchise stores. Mackinac Island fudge, flavored corns, caramel apples and dipped chocolate novelties are usually made at the stores, which also feature hand-dipped ice cream.

Branson's shop can be reached by calling (417) 334-9240; for information about the St. Charles location, call (636) 395-7081.

Northwoods Candy Emporium, www.northwoodscandy.com

A touch of the Great Northwest is the theme of these candy franchises. In Branson, guests are greeted at the door with a water feature that's supposed to suggest a mountain waterfall and a toy train that circles around the store's ceiling. A small candy-making demonstration area turns out creamy fudge or dipped treats, such as jumbo marshmallow-chocolate lollipops. The peanut butter-chocolate fudge was yummy, but I wasn't adventurous enough to try citrus-soda-flavored fudge.

In addition to the Branson Landing location, another store is in Springfield's Battlefield Mall. Corporate offices also are in Branson. Other Northwoods stores are in Minnesota and North Dakota.

Contact the Branson store at (417) 332-1010; Springfield, (417) 708-8800.

Rocky Mountain Chocolate Factory, www.rockymountainchocolatefactory.com

Rocky Mountain Chocolate has franchise stores in the United States, Canada and the United Arab Emirates. Based in Durango, Colo., which is home to its 53,000-square-foot factory, the company produces 300 different chocolate candies and confectionary products.

Look for Rocky Mountain Chocolate in these Missouri cities: Branson, Kansas City, Osage Beach, St. Charles and St. Joseph. Individual stores prepare a variety of caramel and candy apples, fudge, chocolate items and confections in full view of the customer using traditional cooking utensils such as copper kettles on gas-fired stoves and marble slab cooling tables.

The Fudgery, www.fudgeryfudge.com

Placing its stores in locations with heavy tourist foot traffic is the business model for this national chain. The other component is mixing up a good deal of fun into each batch of fudge. As onlookers gather around, employees make fudge from scratch, explaining a little about the candy-making process while throwing in some good-natured silliness.

The Fudgery got its start in the Outerbanks of North Carolina in 1980. In Missouri, tourists can find The Fudgery at Branson Landing, as well as at Branson's Tanger Outlet Mall. Two locations are in St. Louis: Ballpark Village across the street from Busch Stadium and at Saint Louis Union Station.

Wine Not?

Missouri chocolate and wine pair beautifully

The outside thermometer reads 94 degrees, but couples and small groups of friends fill the sprawling decks at Chandler Hill Vineyards in Defiance, Mo. Chilled wine, lively conversation, and a magnificent view of the vineyards and valley make this warm Missouri Sunday over Labor Day weekend easier to bear. Inside, the cool, massive tasting room bustles with customers.

Chocolate and fine wine is one of those perfect pairings, and if you are already indulging in Missouri-made chocolate, you'll be happy to hear the Show-Me State has more than 120 wineries that offer just the right vintage to complement your favorite sweet.

Did you know that the country's first federally approved American Viticultural Area (AVA) was granted to Missouri? Augusta, Mo., near Defiance was named an AVA on June 20, 1980, eight months before California's Napa Valley became the country's second AVA.

In total, there are four AVAs in Missouri – Ozark Mountain, Hermann and Ozark Highlands – and 10 wine trails. The soil and rolling hills in Missouri's river valleys reminded European settlers of home, and they soon discovered grapes could grow in this new land. Several varietals are grown in Missouri, although the state grape is the Norton.

Like its chocolatiers, Missouri vintners go about their award-winning work without a lot of fanfare. Chandler Hill, for example, has consistently won gold, silver and bronze medals in statewide competitions. In Hermann, Mo., Stone Hill Winery – which dates to 1847 – won national and international medals prior to Prohibition. In recent years, its stellar Norton red has won national awards. These are just two of the fine wineries that call Missouri home.

Port-style wines from Hermannhof Winery in Hermann and West Winery in Macon, Mo., both received silver medals in the 2015 Finger Lakes International Wine Competition.

Augusta Winery's Estate Bottled Vintage Port won gold in the 2015 Mid-American Wine Competition. Silver medals in that competition went to Augusta Winery for its Icewine; Stonehaus Farms (Lee's Summit, Mo.) for its Missouri Port; Adam Puchta Winery (Hermann) for its Signature Port; and Montelle Winery (Augusta) for its Vidal Icewine.

For 20 years, the Missouri Wine and Grape Board has worked tirelessly to show off the Show-Me State's wine industry. Their efforts have helped to make wineries friendly for everybody, not just wine aficionados. Missouri wineries offer tastings, events and tours. Wine-makers welcome questions about what wine goes with certain foods – including chocolate.

Chocolate has its own powerful flavor profiles, so you'll want a sturdy wine to pair with this dessert. The Wine and Grape Board offers these suggestions for chocolate pairings.

Starting with the simplest dessert – pieces of fine, dark chocolate – serve a glass of full-bodied Norton, a dry red wine with overtones of berry and spice to complement the chocolate. Or, offer guests a glass of Concord wine – a sweet, fruity red – with a beautiful chocolate truffle.

Chambourcin (*sham-bor-san*), a balance of dry and sweet, is referred to by the Wine and Grape Board as "a nice gateway to red wines." It pairs well with a slice of chocolate cake for dessert.

A port-style wine always pairs well with any chocolate dessert and can be used when baking with chocolate. This red wine is richer, heavier and has a higher alcohol content. It's often served with chocolate or dried fruits.

Martin Luther is recorded as saying, "Beer is made by men, wine by God." The native people of Central and South America believed chocolate to come from gods. No wonder, then, that these two indulgences go so well together.

Missouri Wine and Grape Board, www.missouriwine.org
P.O. Box 630, Jefferson City, MO, 65102, (800) 392-9463

Stone Hill Winery. Courtesy of Deborah Reinhardt.

Decadent Chocolate Cupcakes with Hazelnut Spread Whipped Frosting

Recipe by Deborah Reinhardt

While I'm not ready for *Cupcake Wars* by any stretch of the imagination, these little beauties are really quite delightful. Take box cake mix to a whole new level with Askinosie Chocolate's Hey, Hey Hazelnut!™ Chocolate Hazelnut Spread. Made from scratch in their Springfield, Mo., factory, this spread is also perfectly wonderful eaten right out of the jar (yes, I have done that).

Ingredients

1 box Duncan Hines Classic Devil's Food cake mix
1 cup water
3 eggs
⅓ cup vegetable oil

Instructions

Preheat oven to 350 degrees (325 degrees for dark or coated pans). Line 2 muffin pans with cupcake liners. Beat ingredients together for two minutes at medium speed. Fill each cupcake liner halfway with the batter. Bake 18 to 21 minutes or until toothpick comes out clean when inserted in middle of a cupcake. Makes 24 cupcakes. Cool on wire racks.

For the chocolate hazelnut cream filling and frosting, add 3 Tablespoons of Askinosie Chocolate's Hey, Hey Hazelnut!™ Chocolate Hazelnut Spread to one 12-ounce can of Betty Crocker Whipped Cream Frosting. Mix by hand until completely blended. If you don't have a pastry bag, make one by making a very small snip off a corner of a plastic sandwich bag. Spoon frosting mixture into the bag and twist gently to bring the mixture to the tip. Using the handle of a wooden mixing spoon, gently poke a hole into the top of each cupcake and squeeze a small amount of the frosting mixture into the hole. Repeat for each cupcake. Using remaining frosting mixture, frost the cupcakes. Garnish with broken bits of your favorite Askinosie chocolate bar.

Make simple cupcakes elegant with chocolate hazelnut spread and broken dark chocolate from Askinosie Chocolate in Springfield, Mo. Courtesy of Deborah Reinhardt.

Cherry Mash Cookies

Recipe courtesy of Chase Candy Company, with thanks to Bonnie Lytton

The aroma of these cookies baking in the oven rivals any scented candle from the shopping mall.

Ingredients

- 2 ¼ cups all-purpose flour
- 1 teaspoon baking soda
- 1 teaspoon salt
- 1 cup butter (two sticks), softened
- ¾ cup granulated sugar
- ¾ cup packed brown sugar
- 1 teaspoon vanilla
- 2 eggs
- 8 small Cherry Mash candy bars, chopped

Instructions

Preheat oven to 375 degrees. Combine flour, baking soda and salt in a small bowl. Beat butter, granulated sugar, brown sugar and vanilla in large mixer bowl. Add eggs, one at a time, beating well after each addition. Gradually beat in flour mixture. Stir in Cherry Mash candy.

Drop by rounded teaspoons onto ungreased baking sheets. Bake for 9 to 11 minutes or until golden brown.

Cool on baking sheets for two minutes before removing to wire racks to cool completely. Makes 18 to 20 large cookies.

Courtesy of Deborah Reinhardt.

Cherry Mash Martini

Recipe courtesy of Chase Candy Company

Here's a perfect Valentine's Day cocktail – it's like a chocolate-covered cherry for adults.

Ingredients

1 ½ ounces EFFEN® black cherry vodka
¾ ounce Disaronno amaretto
¾ ounce créme de cacao
¼ ounce half-and-half

Instructions

Shake vigorously in a shaker with ice. Strain into a martini glass. Garnish with a maraschino cherry and ¼ of a Mini Mash candy bar on a drink pick.

Courtesy of Deborah Reinhardt.

Parisian Hot Chocolate

Recipe courtesy of Elle's Patisserie

Elle Feldman loves all things French, so when it was time to pick a recipe for *le chocolat chaud,* she went to fellow Francophile and cookbook author David Lebovitz. "No reason to reinvent the wheel when this is the best," she says. The patisserie adds a pinch of sea salt, and I'd recommend floating one of Elle's homemade marshmallows on top.

Ingredients

2 cups whole milk

5 ounces bittersweet chocolate, best-quality, finely chopped

2 Tablespoons light brown sugar (optional)

Instructions

Heat the milk in a medium-sized saucepan. Once the milk is warm, whisk in the chocolate, stirring until melted and steaming hot. For a thick hot chocolate, cook at a very low boil for about 3 minutes, whisking constantly. Be careful and keep an eye on the mixture, as it may boil up a bit during the first moments.Taste, and add brown sugar if desired.

Serve warm in small demitasse or coffee cups. Makes four servings.

Note: This hot chocolate improves if made ahead and allowed to sit for a few hours. Rewarm before serving.

Parisian hot chocolate – le chocolat chaud – gets its rich taste and consistency from fine, chopped chocolate, not cream. This recipe uses whole milk. Photo by Antonio Gravante/Fotolia.com.

Chocolate Waffles with Fleur de Sel Caramel Buttercream

Recipe courtesy of Southmoreland on the Plaza

This recipe is adaptable to gluten-free flour as well. Simply replace the flour in the waffle batter with an equal amount of all gluten-free flour. They are equally delicious prepared both ways. This recipe comes from the Southmoreland blog, which can be found on the inn's website, www.southmoreland.com.

Caramel sauce, also used in the buttercream, has a kiss of French sea salt. An elegant breakfast that is served at Southmoreland on the Plaza. Photo by Deborah Reinhardt.

Fleur de Sel Caramel Sauce

¾ cup sugar
½ cup water
¼ cup corn syrup
1 teaspoon vanilla
½ cup heavy cream
2 Tablespoons butter
½ teaspoon Fleur de Sel (French sea salt)

Instructions

In a small sauté pan, combine sugar, water and corn syrup. Cook over medium heat, stirring occasionally until mixture is an amber color. Carefully add vanilla, heavy cream and butter stirring constantly until smooth. Stir in the Fleur de Sel and set aside.

Fleur de Sel Caramel Buttercream

1 ½ cup confectioner's sugar
½ cup butter (softened)
¼ cup Fleur de Sel Caramel Sauce

Instructions

Combine all ingredients in a mixing bowl and whisk until smooth. Spoon into a piping bag fitted with a piping tip, such as Ateco# 806. Set aside.

Chocolate Waffles

1 ½ cups all-purpose flour
½ cup cocoa
2 Tablespoons sugar
1 Tablespoons baking powder
½ teaspoon baking soda
½ teaspoon salt
3 eggs
1 cup milk
½ cup vegetable oil
1 cup semi-sweet chocolate chips

Instructions

Pre-heat the waffle iron according to manufacturer's instructions. Combine dry ingredients in a large mixing bowl and whisk to combine. In a separate bowl, combine wet ingredients and whisk until smooth. Gently fold dry ingredients into the wet ingredients and add chocolate chips. Be careful not to over mix. Ladle the batter onto the hot generously oiled waffle iron and cook. Cut waffles and arrange them on a plate. Pipe buttercream on top and drizzle with Fleur de Sel Caramel Sauce. Serves 4

Chocolate Zucchini Bread

Recipe courtesy of Southmoreland on the Plaza

Kansas City innkeepers Nancy Miller and Mark Reichle had so many recipe requests from guests that they decided to publish a cookbook, *Tried & True: Southmoreland on the Plaza's Recipes by Request*. This recipe for their crazy-good chocolate zucchini bread is one of the recipes featured on the book, which is available for purchase at the inn. Most people never believe the bread has zucchini squash as an ingredient, say Nancy and Mark, who make 10 loaves at a time. Make grating the squash easier by using a food processor's grater attachment. This recipe will make two loaves. Try it for breakfast or just for a sweet snack.

Ingredients

- 3 eggs
- 1 cup vegetable oil
- 2 teaspoons salt
- 2 cups granulated sugar
- 3 cups grated zucchini
- 2 teaspoons cinnamon
- 2 teaspoons baking soda
- ¼ teaspoon baking powder
- 2 teaspoons vanilla
- 2 ⅓ cups flour
- ½ cup unsweetened cocoa

Instructions

Preheat oven to 350 degrees. Sift together all dry ingredients (salt, sugar, cinnamon, baking soda, baking powder, flour and cocoa). In a second bowl, mix together the zucchini, eggs, oil and vanilla. Fold wet mixture into the dry ingredients. Spoon batter into two greased bread pans. Bake for 45 – 60 minutes. (Varying moisture content of zucchini can vary the baking time). Test for doneness with a toothpick at 45 minutes and check again every five minutes until the toothpick comes out clean.

Chocolate zucchini bread is often requested at breakfast by Southmoreland guests. Photo by Nancy Miller.

Meet the Author

Deborah Reinhardt

For more than 30 years, Deborah Reinhardt has worked as a travel writer and editor. She started with newspapers before moving to magazines. As a member of the travel/tourism industry, she has developed a respected reputation, often speaking at conferences. Deborah loves to tell and present stories that spark a spirit of discovery in her readers.

Her job has given her opportunities to travel throughout Missouri, the United States, and several other countries. She says, "Meeting people during these trips has shown me that we're really more alike than different. Travel fosters an understanding that is unmatched in most other activities."

A lifelong resident of St. Louis, Mo., Deborah lives with her "fur family" of dogs and cats, who seem intent on distracting her from working in her home office. She has one daughter who is currently attending a Missouri university.

Join the conversation about chocolate, travel, and other inspiring topics by following Deborah's blog, which can be found at www.DeborahReinhardt.com.

Other ways to connect include:

Facebook: www.facebook.com/DelectableDestinations
Pinterest: www.pinterest.com/drpstl
Twitter: @ GirlPowerPub

Index

Recipe Index